The
KENSINGTON
BOOK

First published 2006
by Historical Publications Ltd
32 Ellington Street, London N7 8PL
(Tel: 020 7607 1628)

ISBN 1-905286-16-3
British Library Cataloguing-in-Publication Data
A catalogue record for this book is available from the British Library

Reproduction by Gilderson's, Pitfield Street, London N1
Printed in Zaragoza, Spain by Edelvives

The Illustrations

The following have kindly given permission to reproduce illustrations:

Central Press: *127*
Roger Cline: *4, 5, 15, 16, 17, 18, 26, 47, 70, 80, 128*
Getty Images: *121*
Royal Borough of Kensington and Chelsea: *3, 10, 27, 33, 34, 42, 45, 49, 56, 60, 66, 73, 75, 88, 91, 99, 107, 108, 110, 112, 117, 118, 119, 122, 129, 132, 133, 136, 137, 138, 140, 144, 156, 157, 158, 160, 168 and the front cover*
Linley Sambourne House, London, UK/Bridgeman Art Library: *106*
London Metropolitan Archives: *53*
National Monuments Record: *62*
National Portrait Gallery: *12, 28, 57, 103*
National Trust: *125*
John Rogers: *59 and the back cover*
Richard Tames: *23*
V & A Images, Victoria & Albert Museum: *130*

It has not been possible to trace the copyright or reproduction right ownership of illustrations 82 (Georgette Heyer) and John Millais (114). The publisher invites those concerned to apply to them so that due acknowledgement may be made in any future printings.

Other images were supplied by the Publisher.

The KENSINGTON BOOK

Carolyn Starren

HISTORICAL PUBLICATIONS

Introduction

Local history is, for many people, an endlessly fascinating subject and one that is constantly evolving as it is as much a study of the present as of the past. It becomes even more interesting if you are personally involved. Although I was born and raised in Chelsea, my scholastic and much of my working life has been spent in southern Kensington the area covered by this book. In the following pages I hope to give a flavour of the buildings, business, institutions but above all the people that have created this exciting and vibrant area of the Royal Borough of Kensington and Chelsea.

This volume fills the gap between the *Notting Hill and Holland Park Book* and the *Chelsea Book* thus completing the story of the Royal Borough. Although the area covered is small – from High Street Kensington in the north to Fulham Road in the south and from Knightsbridge in the east via South Kensington and Brompton to Earl's Court in the west – there is much of local and national interest to be discovered. A short stroll in any direction shows that southern Kensington is primarily a Victorian creation. Prior to 1850, nurseries and market gardens predominated with a scattering of elegant squares, terraces and villas, by the end of the 1870s the whole area was covered by bricks and mortar.

It is impossible to do full justice to this fascinating area in 128 pages, after all the *Survey of London* required three volumes to cover the architectural history. Certain topics and themes could not be ignored such as Kensington Palace, arts and culture, exhibitions and shopping but many of the other items included are more personal choices. Compiling this book has taken me on a wonderful journey down memory lane. The years spent at Wetherby's with Mrs Lloyd Webber as music teacher and nativity plays at St Augustine's, then on to Queen's Gate School and the twice weekly walk in a long crocodile to Kensington Gardens when it was fine and the museums when it rained, plays at Baden Powell House and later forbidden lunches in local hostelries. When I joined the Borough's library service in 1968, too much of my munificent salary of £45.00 a month was spent in Biba, Kensington Market, the Troubadour and the Paris Pullman among others.

I greatly missed collaborating with the late Barbara Denny, but I was able to draw on her extensive knowledge via her library and papers. I am very grateful to Clair Drever for her help with research and drafting parts of the text, without her assistance this project would not have been possible.

Carolyn Starren
September 2006

Text in bold type indicates a separate entry

Abbots of Abingdon

Abingdon in Berkshire appears to be an odd starting point for a book on Kensington but the association goes back to the 11th century.

At the time of the Norman Conquest the Manor of Kensington was given to Geoffrey, Bishop of Coutances who in turn passed it to Aubrey de Vere in 1093. The de Veres, who later became the Earls of Oxford, were to retain the Manor for the next 500 years. However, Godfrey de Vere gave a small area around the old chapel of St Mary to the Abbey of Abingdon in 1100 in thanks for their care of his son during a serious illness. This gift became known as the Abbots Manor and its church as **St Mary Abbots**.

The name of the new owners of the Abbots Manor is commemorated in several street names including Abingdon Road. In the Swinging '60s this became an important location when the very first **Biba** opened here in a derelict former chemist's shop. Two large mansion flats, Abingdon Court and Abingdon Gardens, were completed in the first years of the twentieth century. The former had hydraulic lifts powered by the London Hydraulic Power Company which had a 184-mile network of pipes under London.

Adam and Eve Mews

The Adam and Eve pub in Kensington High Street originally stood in a large garden and when it was put up for auction in 1765 the notice boasted of "a

1. *Richard Brinsley Sheridan, a frequent visitor to the Adam and Eve.*

delightful view towards Holland House and from the rear a prospect to Surrey". In those days Richard Sheridan was a frequent visitor, doubtless on his way to visit his friend Charles James Fox at Holland House. First rebuilt in 1823, it was moved in 1882 to the west side of the mews to 163 Kensington High Street. Famed for its dining room, a favourite with **G K Chesterton**, the pub's closure in 1972 was mourned by many.

Meanwhile the row of cottages behind was changed into a mews and some of the stables used to house police horses. The Middlesex Rifles also had a drill hall here. In Edwardian days, Kensington's first cinema, the Royalty, with a narrow entrance foyer at 177 Kensington High Street, extended back into the mews. They served tea and biscuits, included in the ticket price, to its matinée audiences.

The mews suffered severe damage early in 1940 when a bomb destroyed the cinema together with Long's Buildings, a 19th-century stable block converted into small dwellings. The site remained vacant or used as a car park until new houses were built in 1985.

Airships

There was considerable excitement in 1855 when the dockyard of the Royal Aeronautical Society in Victoria Road, opposite **Kensington Gardens**, became the first 'London Airport'. An announcement was made that the first aerial ship, the Eagle, measuring 160 feet long, 50 feet high and 40 feet wide and manned by a crew of seventeen experimental sailors would leave for Paris.

It was described as a "stupendous first rate man-of-war, containing 2400 yards of oil silk on a 75-foot frame, with a 6-foot wide cabin suspended in the centre by ropes." It was to be steered by an immense rudder and four flappers. Future voyages were planned to Vienna, Berlin and St Petersburg, but actually the dirigible never left the ground and provided comedians with material for months.

Albertopolis

First coined in the 1856, the term Albertopolis is once again appearing in the press in connection with plans to improve the area and seek World Heritage site status. When the **Great Exhibition** was opened in 1851 on a site between Alexandra Gate and the Knightsbridge barracks, much of the surrounding area consisted of market and horticultural gardens with a scattering of country estates. Following its success, the profits were used to purchase the 87-acre site south of Hyde Park by the **Royal Commission for the Exhibition of 1851** to be developed as a centre for culture and learning.

Prince Albert's vision slowly evolved in the area he christened South Kensington. The Prince

2. *Prince Albert, from the painting by Winterhalter, 1855.*

3. *The Bell and Horns, which stood where Thurloe Place joins Brompton Road, on the Alexander Estate.*

opened the first venture, the **Royal Horticultural Gardens**, in June 1861 and was involved with plans for the **1862 Exhibition** when he fell ill and died shortly after. Others took up the challenge to implement Prince Albert's grand scheme. Very quickly the great museums, the **Natural History Museum**, South Kensington Museum (later renamed the **Victoria & Albert**), The Imperial Institute (later the **Commonwealth Institute**) and the **Science** and Geological **Museum** opened as did the **Royal Colleges** of Science, Mines, Naval Architecture and Engineering, Art and **Needlework**. There were also National Schools of Cookery and of Art and Woodcarving and Imperial College of Science and Technology. Music was not forgotten with the Royal Albert Hall, the Royal College of Music and the **Royal College of Organists** completing the list. Although some no longer exist and others have amalgamated, a magnificent legacy remains the largest concentration of internationally renowned museums and colleges in the world.

Alexander Estate

The Alexander or Thurloe Estate, comprising 54 acres in six lots, has a complex, often colourful history. A quick synopsis of the facts helps to dispel the myth that Oliver Cromwell gave the estate to his spymaster John Thurloe. As with the **Harrington Estate** the story begins with Sir William Blake. In addition to Hale House land, Blake also owned Harrison's Nursery, now Alexander and Thurloe Square, William Attwood's market garden which sat on twenty acres around Gloucester Road station area and land north of Brompton Road.

In 1760 Harris Thurloe Brace inherited the estate from his mother, Anna Maria Harris, a descendant of Sir William Blake, who married John Thurloe Brace, a grandson of John Thurloe in 1713. When Harris

4. *Alexander Square looking north. The left hand block is dated 1827, that on the right 1830.*

5. The east side of Thurloe Square, from a lithograph by Madeley.

6. Princess Alice, from a photograph by Mayall.

Brace died without a direct heir, he left the estate to John Alexander, a lawyer, who was related through Anna Maria's first marriage.

While it is true that the Braces were related to John Thurloe, the lands came via the female line and there is the small matter of a slight discrepancy in dates between 1640s and the 1713 marriage of Anna Maria and John Thurloe Brace. But then facts have never been allowed to spoil a good story.

It fell to Alexander's son, Henry Browne Alexander, to develop the estate over the next fifty years. The successors to Basevi and Bonin, creators of the Alexander and Thurloe Square area, were Thomas Cundy III, Charles Aldin and his sons, William Jackson, John Spicer and **Ernest George and Peto**. Between them from 1851 to the 1880s they were responsible for constructing Queen's Gate Gardens, Ashburn Gardens, Place and Mews, Courtfield Road, 104-156 Gloucester Road (including **Bailey's Hotel** and **St Stephen's Church**), Southwell Gardens and Harrington Gardens.

Henry's son, William, is best known for the £80,000 he gave to pay for the National Portrait Gallery's present building and for the donation of family portraits including that of John Thurloe. A bachelor to the end, his estate passed to his cousin, Sybil, who was married to Lord George Campbell, son of the 8th Duke of Argyll. What now remains of the estate is held in trust by the Anstruther family.

Princess Alice, Countess of Athlone

The Duchess of Albany, the former Princess Helena Frederica of Waldeck, widow of Victoria's youngest son, Leopold and her daughter, Princess Alice, moved into **Kensington Palace** in 1917.

Princess Alice (1883-1981), as did many other aunts and female relatives, lived in the Clock House, the so-called 'Aunt Heap', for much of her life. It is not known exactly who first coined the phrase, but many credit the Duke of Windsor. Princess Alice herself refers to it in her journals.

When Princess Alice died in 1981 a Memorial Fund was set up by the **Kensington Society** and an avenue of beech trees was planted in front of Kensing-

ton Palace in her memory. A garden was also created by the Society in the forecourt of the new Civic Centre. This includes Myrtle grown from a cutting of the bush from which a sprig was cut for Queen Victoria's wedding bouquet. The garden was the work of Fred Nutbeam, a gardener at Buckingham Palace.

Princess Alice, Duchess of Gloucester, who died at the venerable age of 102 in 2004, an aunt of the current monarch, also lived in 'Aunt Heap' in the latter years of her life.

Allen Family

Complicated questions of ownership prevented the development of the south side of Kensington High Street west of the **Adam and Eve**. In 1801 a ten-acre site was split up and sold to various developers. The most prominent of these was Thomas Allen, a tailor and breaches maker of Old Bond Street, who is said to have made most of his very considerable fortune supplying uniforms during the

Napoleonic Wars. His son, Thomas Newland Allen, named after one of his father's country estates, together with the rest of the Allen family, was associated with this part of Kensington for well over a century. Allen's solicitor William à Beckett, believed to have been the model for Dickens' Ralph Nickleby, was reputedly quick tempered and quarrelsome.

After the fashion of the time, their developments on the main road were divided into terraces which included Newland Terrace and Newland Place. All the houses were fairly large, set back from the road, with long gardens behind and from the first attracted wealthy residents. In his earliest days of ownership, the first Thomas Allen formed two streets southward, first Newland Street (now Abingdon Road), followed shortly after by Allen Street. Allen House, a block of very large mansion flats, in the 1980s became one of the area's first timeshare blocks. The flats multiplied by subdivision, a controversial development that engendered much anxiety.

Field Marshal Edmund Allenby

Edmund Allenby (1861-1936) was born in Nottinghamshire and attended Haileybury and Sandhurst. He joined the Inniskillings as an officer and first saw active service in South Africa during the Boer War.

He led the First Cavalry division in the retreat from Mons and was commander at the first battle of Ypres during the early stages of First World War. Following promotion he went on to lead the Third Army most

7. *Field Marshal Allenby (left) with his wife and Lord Carnarvon at the site of the excavation of the tomb of Tutankhamen in which Carnarvon was involved (see Howard Carter).*

notably at the Battle of Arras in 1917. Although, unlike many of his contemporaries, Allenby was shown to be a brilliant commander, personally he suffered a tragic loss when his only son was killed in action that year.

Command of the Egyptian Expeditionary Force followed where he was charged to regain Palestine. He employed a variety of tactics which included utilising the skills of T E Lawrence in the desert skirmishes, brilliantly recreated in David Lean's film *Lawrence of Arabia*. Allenby led the last major cavalry battle at Megiddo where the Turkish army was heavily defeated.

After a brief spell as Special High Commissioner for Egypt he resigned in 1925 taking up residency at 24 Wetherby Gardens in 1928, where he built a splendid aviary in the garden.

The Art Fund

Many houses in South Kensington can boast of having an artist in residence at one time or another. There is one house that since construction has always been associated with the arts, 7 Cromwell Place. The first occupant was **John Millais**, followed by the portrait painters James Archer and Herman Schiechen; the next residents were photographers including Emil Otta Hoppe and Anthony Gordon, then **Francis Bacon** from 1943 to 1952 and finally Robert Buhler RA.

In 1993 Millais House, as it was now called, became the headquarters of the Art Fund. Millais' studio is now the boardroom. The charity was founded in 1903 to save art that would otherwise leave the country or disappear into private collections, for presentation to public galleries. Whistler's *Nocturne in Blue and Gold* was the first work to be saved. Since then the fund has help to acquire over 850,000 works of art.

Artists' studios

The traditional image of the struggling artist in an attic had all but died by the mid-nineteenth century. A successful Victorian artist could be an affluent one and nowhere was this more evident than in Kensington. Supported by wealthy patrons and commanding good prices for their work, artists built magnificent studio homes. The key features were large north-facing windows which gave the best light for painting and entertaining space as befitted their new found status. The most famous group in Kensington is the artists' colony in Holland Park, where at one time no fewer than six Royal Academicians resided including the President, Frederick Lord Leighton.

But these were by no means the only example. Others include Millais' house at 2 Palace Gate, Richard Ansdell at 1 St Alban's Grove and Victoria Road and 4-28 (even) Yeoman's Row. These houses have been well documented but less attention has been paid to the construction of multiple studios, often erected as part of speculative development. Studio blocks can be found on every estate but probably the best and most interesting example is Avenue Studios in Sydney Mews built by Sir Charles Freake.

Originally built as stables and workshops it was used by Baron Carlo Marochetti, the sculptor. His pupil, C E Hallé, recalled that Landseer's lions for Trafalgar Square were cast here by Marochetti. After the sculptor's death the studio was converted in the 1870s into a number of studios ranged either side of an arched corridor. Those on the south side were three storeys

8. Two occupants of Avenue Studios. Above, Edward Poynter and below (9) John Singer Sargent.

high with large windows and skylights to admit north light, while those on the other side facing north have two storeys. The success of this enterprise is very apparent from the list of eminent artists who worked here. They were C E Hallé, **Joseph Edgar Boehm**, Frank Dicey, John Wills Good, Charles Lutyens, Edward J Poynter, Alfred Gilbert, John Singer Sargent, Philip Wilson Steer, George Edward Wade and John Tweed.

Laura Ashley

The first shop under the Laura Ashley name opened in Pelham Street, South Kensington, in 1968. Laura Ashley (1925-1985) created a distinctive 'look' for women as well as home fabrics that signalled a return to a fresher less industrial world. Laura was born Laura Mountney in Dowlais, Merthyr Tydfil. She met Bernard Ashley at a youth club in Wallington, and they married in 1949. Working from their kitchen in Pimlico, Laura and Bernard peddled her wares by going around to the leading stores and by mail order. She died in 1985, but her husband Bernard carried on the company that bears her name. 'Laura Ashley' is not as popular as it used to be but still maintains a presence in the fashion world.

Asylums

A number of the large houses in Kensington during the late 18th and early 19th centuries were taken over and used as asylums. Examples include Earl's Court House where Mary Bradbury established a private asylum for young ladies of a nervous disposition and Cowper House on the south side of the Old Brompton Road.

Kensington House, on the site of what is now the east end of Kensington Court, was taken in 1830 by William C Finch, a member of the Royal College of Surgeons for use as an asylum. He was already running a similar establishment in Chelsea. The prospectus described "enlightened moral and mental treatment, a library, billiard room, music and the benefits of religion, not neglected, pleasure

Two major houses which became Asylums. Above (10) is Earl's Court House and below (11) is the first Kensington House in 1776, to be demolished later for a much grander mansion (see Albert Grant).

12. Francis Bacon, oil painting by Ruskin Spear, 1984.
© National Portrait Gallery, London

grounds and comfortable apartments from 21 to 30 shillings a week." A very different account, however, was given by Richard Paternoster, who had been forcibly confined there in 1838. He wrote of his ordeal firstly in the *Satirist* and secondly in a book *The Madhouse System*. Here he wrote of brutal keepers, overcrowding, scanty and bad food, no amusements, books, baths or medical treatment.

The asylum changed hands in 1840 and prospered under the new proprietor, Dr Francis Philp. He retired in 1852 but kept the freehold of Kensington House while still residing at Colby House next door. Twenty years later he sold both houses to **Baron Albert Grant**.

Francis Bacon

Francis Bacon (1909-1992) lived at 7 Cromwell Place, once home to **Sir John Millais**, now home to the **Art Fund** which helps to save works of art for the nation. Irish born Bacon did not attend art school but became one of the most internationally renowned painters of the 20th century. Initially working as an interior designer in the 1930s, he devoted himself exclusively to painting from 1944. During this time he lived at 7 Cromwell Place. A rebel all his life he was a member of the hard drinking Soho crowd in the 1950s. Often regarded as a self-destructive genius he frequently destroyed his own work and could be violent both on canvas and in life.

His most famous address in the Royal Borough was 7 Reece Mews, his studio-cum-bedsit for thirty years. On his death the studio was left to his long term lover, John Edwards. Access was given to the photographer Perry Ogden who produced a fascinating record of the studio Bacon worked in every day from dawn to midday. Full of clutter and mess, even the doors and windows had been used as palettes. It remained untouched until 1998 when Edwards donated it to the Hugh Lane Gallery in Dublin and it was dismantled piece by piece to be re-constructed in Dublin and went on display on 23 May 2001.

Lord Robert Baden Powell

Robert Baden Powell (1857-1941) spent much of his childhood at 9 Hyde Park Gate and later at 32 Princes Gate. It was his role in the defence of Mafeking during the Boer War that first brought him fame and on his return he moved into Princes Gate. During his time in

13. *Lord Robert Baden Powell, from a water colour by Ape Junior in* Vanity Fair.

14. *Bailey's Hotel c.1905. Designed by Aldin & Sons, it was opened in 1876.*

South Africa he began to formulate his plans for an organisation for youth which eventually became the Boy Scouts. The movement began in 1907 with a camp for 20 boys on Brownsea Island, Poole Harbour, Dorset. He published *Scouting for Boys* in 1908 which was followed by a further 30 books. Baden Powell was World Chief Scout from 1920 until his death and, with his sister Agnes, founded the Girl Guides in 1910. His young wife Olave, whom he married in 1912, became Chief Commissioner for the Girl Guides in 1916 and devoted the rest of her life to the organisation. Created a baron in 1929, Baden Powell retired in 1938 and with Olave moved to Kenya where he died in 1941.

The Scouts' Association's headquarters is based in Baden Powell House at the junction of **Queen's Gate** and **Cromwell Road**, where a life-size statue of Baden Powell stands outside. Today the organisation boasts some 28 million members in all corners of the globe.

Bailey's Hotel, Gloucester Road

Recently restored to its former Victorian glory, Bailey's Hotel sits in the tourist heartland of Kensington and dates back to 1876. It retains much of its Victorian heritage with sweeping staircases, stained glass windows and real fireplaces.

The hotel was purpose built adjacent to Gloucester Road Station. James Bailey, originally from Norfolk, lived on the premises with his family and a live-in staff of thirty-five. He believed that the enterprise should "in all respects be conducted in the most respectable manner". It appears to have been a success, as the premises were extended three times between 1877 and 1883. Electricity and lifts were introduced in the 1890s

These 'elevators' were especially targeted at the American market who generally did not hold a high opinion of English hotels. A contemporary guidebook assured transatlantic travellers that they would find themselves in "rich and substantial surroundings" with the most up-to-date sanitation, stringent fire precautions, and an excellent wine cellar but also with a "cosy, homelike, atmosphere". The hotel still continues to thrive and entertain American tourists.

Barker's store

The once great department store closed its doors for good in January 2006 – however, one can still marvel at this beautiful example of Art-Deco architecture, as its listed status safeguards it from demolition. The archives of the store, and the people associated with it, are kept in the House of Fraser Group Archive at the University of Glasgow.

John Barker was born in Kent on 6 April 1840 and by the 1860s

17. A delivery tricycle used by Barker's before the 1st World War.

15. Sir John Barker, founder of the store, depicted in Vanity Fair.

he was working with William Whiteley the famous store owner in Westbourne Grove. When the promised partnership failed to materialize he joined up with James Whitehead and together they purchased two newly built shops at 91 and 93 Kensington High Street. Both the premises and merchandise sold prolifer-ated and by 1887 *The Queen* described Barker's as "the best establishment in London for moderate prices". The empire consisted of 28 shops, a staff of over a thousand and a delivery

16. This mammoth cheese was displayed at an exhibition at Wembley in 1924. It was then delivered to Barker's for resale.

18. A poster advertising Christmas goods in 1879.

and post-war building restrictions but finally in 1958 the project was completed.

In July 1957 the House of Fraser made a successful take over bid. From that time the slow disintegration of the mighty Barker's empire began until the final chapter was reached in January 2006.

Syd Barrett

Psychedelia, acid and rock are not normally words used in connection with famous Kensington residents but are in the case of the tortured musical genius, Syd Barrett, co-founder of Pink Floyd.

Roger Keith Barrett (1946-2006) was born in Cambridge. He met Roger Waters and others associated with the Pink Floyd phenomenon at Cambridge High School. When Syd arrived in London he moved into a flat at 101 Gloucester Road which he shared with a bright, druggie clique from his home town. Becoming alarmed by Syd's drug taking, his manager moved him to Egerton Court opposite South Kensington Station. Alas it was too late, Syd was already en route to self destruction. Stories abound about the excesses that took place in Egerton Court, often dismissed by those who did live there. Visitors included Pete Townshend, Mick Jagger and Marianne Faithful.

Following his split with Pink Floyd, Syd moved into Wetherby Mansions, Earl's Court Square with artist Duggie Fields in 1966. Ironically Dave Gilmour, who had replaced him as the band's front man, lived next door. The photographer, Mick Rock was also a flatmate. His iconic pictures of Syd, just before his breakdown, are amongst his

service with twenty horses.

By 1900 the whole section between Young Street and Derry Street was filled and a magnificent new store erected including a food hall. Barker's tentacles then spread across to the north side of the High Street where a furniture department was opened. While Barker's prospered their rivals were not faring so well and in 1907 **Pontings** was taken over, followed by a merger with **Derry and Toms** a few years later.

By then Barker's was in the hands of Sydney Skinner and **Trevor Bowen**, as John Barker had died in 1914. Together, they planned a complete rebuild of all their stores embracing the latest ideas and designs from America. In 1924 the newly qualified architect Bernard George was appointed and he started work immediately on the Derry and Toms building. The ambitious programme was dogged by disputes, controversy, the Second World War

earliest intimate portraits of Rock legends. They were taken both inside and outside the flat, the latter showing Syd's distinctive car, a 1950s' pink Pontiac Parisienne convertible. "Magnetic and edgy, provocative, stimulating and fun, but even then already both wanting to be the focus of attention, and needing to stay behind a locked door to escape it" is how Duggie Fields remembers Syd. Duggie was studying at Chelsea Art College at the time and still lives in the flat. Today, Syd's room is his studio. Syd left the flat in autumn 1968 leaving all his possessions inside; he simply shut the bedroom door and returned home to Cambridge.

Playing under the name Tea Set, Pink Floyd's first commercial gig in February 1965 was at the Countdown Club, 1a Palace Gate. The club, situated in the basement, relied on acts bringing along their friends who hopefully would spend money at the bar. Playing from 9.00pm till 2.00am the band relied on extended solos to augment their small, at this time, repertoire. This was to become the defining feature of Pink Floyd's stage performances. After a few nights a noise injunction was served so they switched to acoustic instruments.

Syd's final legacy to the band was their new name, Pink Floyd Sound, after a blues record he owned featuring two bluesmen from Georgia, Pink Anderson and Floyd Council.

James Barrie

Barrie (1860-1937) lived close to Kensington Gardens and it was here that he first met the **Llewellyn-Davies boys**, George,

19. *James Barrie on the occasion of a school production of one of his own books.*

Jack, Michael and Peter. He described their mother as "the most beautiful creature I had ever seen" and soon he was a frequent visitor to their house where he would tell the boys stories. One of these tales was about the youngest boy, Peter, who, according to Barrie, would one day fly away to Kensington Gardens so that he might be a boy forever. When children died, Peter would take them on a journey to a place called Never Never Land. When George heard the story, he said that "dying must be an awfully big adventure!" Barrie wrote the words down. They would later become the most famous words spoken in Peter Pan.

James Barrie lived at 133 Gloucester Walk between 1895 and 1902 with his wife Mary and their large St Bernard, Porthos, who was the inspiration for Nana, the Darling's canine nanny. He also used rooms in the house as settings for many scenes in the play. This included the first floor bedroom where Peter Pan flew in through the

bay window to take the children to Never Never Land. The house, including the interiors, has been largely preserved by its present owners.

Bela Bartok

Hungarian composer Bela Bartok (1881-1945) regularly stayed at 7 Sydney Place with his friends the Wilsons whenever he was performing in London. His *First Violin Sonata*, performed on the occasion of his first visit to London in 1922, was dismissed by a leading critic as the "last (for the present) in ugliness and incoherence." Subsequent opinion has been more positive, his string quartets in particular being met with appreciation and admiration.

Bartok received his first piano training from his mother. A patriot, he also loved the whole of Eastern Europe, especially its music. However, he was forced to leave after his mother's death in 1939 due to the War. He settled in the USA where he lived unhappily until his death, never

20. Bela Bartok.

21. Chariot racing at Batty's Hippodrome.

giving up his dream of returning home.

Istvan Thomas, a pupil of Listz, also trained Bartok and he counted Listz as a major influence on his music. Other influences included Wagner, Strauss and Debussy but his real inspiration was Hungarian folk music. He collected and classified Hungarian, Slovak, Balkan, Romanian and near Eastern melodies while working as Professor of Piano at Budapest Academy and at Harvard. His folk song collections are amongst his best work. Other famous pieces include his opera *Duke Bluebeard's Castle* and ballets, *The Wooden Prince* and *The Miraculous Mandarin*.

A statue of him stands pensively outside South Kensington tube station.

Batty's Hippodrome

Established by William Batty, a circus proprietor, it was one of the entertaining sideshows of the **Great Exhibition**. Situated between what is now Victoria Road and Palace Gate, it was intended to attract the overflow crowds from Hyde Park.

The Lady's Newspaper of 31 May 1851 wrote about "incredible feats of French equestriennes, probably the best horsewomen in the world" taking part in chariot races and two young Arabs riding ostriches, "the birds have a marvellous speed and are trained admirably." Brass bands played and other events included a monkey's steeplechase. All this took place in an oval arena open to the sky, surrounded by eight rows of seats advertised to accommodate 14,000 people, although probably the actual capacity was much less. There was also a riding school at the south end, which continued for about twenty years after the Hippodrome closed in 1852.

Beauchamp Place

During the 1970s, Beauchamp Place was regarded as one of the best shopping streets in London boasting some of the most illustrious names in British fashion. The rich and famous came to shop and be seen. Although at one time better known for its brothels and common lodging houses, since Edwardian times high fashion boutiques and antique shops proliferated. In the 1950s and '60s it was a mecca for young girls visiting either the Doll's Hospital or the shop selling beautifully crafted horses complete with all possible accessories.

Today, it has been superseded by Sloane Street but still attracts major names such as Caroline Charles, Bruce Oldfield and Janet Reger. Probably the best known restaurant is San Lorenzo's at no. 22, Princess Diana's favourite and still a popular celebrity hangout. A street fair is organised annually by all the local businesses.

On 26 October 1989 Beauchamp Place once again featured in the news when four Georgian houses in the street spectacularly collapsed. During building work tons of masonry and scaffolding fell into the street much to the consternation of onlookers.

Biba

The Biba story is legend – integral to the Swinging '60s. The designer Barbara Hulnacki and her husband Stephen Fitzsimmon were a fundamental part of the '60s fashion scene and included 'Beautiful People' such as Twiggy and other fashionistas. There was no snobbery though, and anyone who loved the purplish and muddy green colours, were free to frequent the shop whatever their social status. They also introduced communal changing areas due to the lack of space, so customers had to be particularly confident when using their premises.

The shop started in a humble, rather derelict chemist's shop on the Abingdon Road. It didn't even have its name above the door. Barbara introduced a fashionable shabby genteel look, in which old was mixed with new. When they outgrew the chemist shop, they trundled their wares over to Church Street, where the old grocery, Nicholls Stores, was vacant. Their next move was to Neal's shoe shop Kensington High Street and then even more ambitiously into the unused **Derry & Toms**, the Art Deco building across the road.

Sadly for its bold entrepreneurs, more people came to look and admire rather than to buy and in two years it had closed, to be replaced by the more down to earth Marks & Spencer and British Home Stores.

Sir Joseph Edgar Boehm

Born in Vienna, of Hungarian descent, Boehm (1834-1890) came to London in 1848 and studied for three years mainly in

22. Sir Joseph Boehm

the British Museum. He settled in London in 1862, acquiring British nationality in 1865. He quickly established himself and received a constant flow of commissions for public monuments, portrait statues and busts. Several of his statues were erected in Kensington including Lord Holland's statue in Holland Park and Lord Napier in Queen's Gate. He also was responsible for Thomas Carlyle's statue on Chelsea Embankment. Boehm lived at several addresses in Kensington including 78 Cornwall Gardens and he worked from Avenue Studios in Sydney Mews.

He became Sculptor in Ordinary to Queen Victoria and taught **Princess Louise**, Victoria's artistic sixth child, at South Kensington Art School. Rumours circulated that Boehm was her lover and the Princess was hastily married to the Marquess of Lorne in 1873 and packed off to Canada. By 1880 the royal couple had separated though they continued to live at Kensington Palace. Boehm and the Princess continued to work to-

23. Terra-cotta sculptures outside Boehm's house in Wetherby Gardens.

gether until he died of a burst blood vessel while alone with her in his Fulham Road studio. Not surprisingly, this caused a press scandal, although Louise insisted that he had collapsed while carrying a heavy bust that brought about a heart aneurism. This was also the Coroner's verdict.

The Boltons

Built as the centre piece of the **Gunter Estate** in the 1850s, this is one of the most exclusive and expensive addresses in London. David Bowie used to live here, and the Sultan of Brunei, one of the world's richest men, still does. Other famous inhabitants have included **W S Gilbert**, Benjamin Golding, founder of the Charing Cross Hospital, **S Carter Hall**, the editor of *Art Journal* and **Douglas Fairbanks jnr**.

On Wednesday, 17 April 1996 an IRA bomb went off at no. 2: luckily it exploded in a

24. *The Boltons, c.1905, with St Mary's church.*

vacant house and there were no casualties. The Boltons is, however, generally a peaceful area without obvious signs of security such as gated areas but thanks in part to the presence of a number of men in black suits and dark glasses.

Charles Booth

Booth (1840-1916), the doyen of social investigators, lived at 6 Grenville Place. It was here that he started work on *Life and Labour of the People in London*, the prototype of the modern social survey. His painstaking work mapped the distribution of poverty throughout the metropolis and revealed how deceptive appearances could be. There were streets classified as 'well to do' which remained in the same family for many years. Whereas other streets, although they looked grander and could be called 'wealthy', were in fact no longer as they seemed: "Houses are now occupied, now empty;

25. *Charles Booth, tireless investigator of London's social inequalities.*

tenants come and go". He obviously thought renting out to lodgers was not very salubrious, as he concludes "Against its downfall each street struggles in vain. Those who can afford to do so leave the stricken district". He also did not think much of

Earl's Court as he cuttingly says, "the tide of fashion and favour which for some time flowed towards Brompton exhausted itself in the Wild West of Earl's Court."

Bousfield School

Built on the site of **Beatrix Potter's** home, Bousfield School is one of the best known state primary schools in Kensington. It is a heavily oversubscribed and popular school and achieved Beacon status in 2001.

During the Second World War, 2 Bolton Gardens, Beatrix Potter's home from 1866 to 1913, was destroyed by a bomb. The bomb crater was cleverly transformed by the architect into an outdoor arena, but sadly, owing to health and safety concerns it can no longer be used. On the open brick exterior wall there is a sign commemorating Beatrix Potter. An official blue plaque cannot be placed here as the original house no longer exists.

Bousfield Primary School was opened in 1956. It is one of the first examples of post war architecture to be made a listed building by English Heritage.

However the original school, named Gloucester Grove East School, was opened in April 1881 in Clareville Street. The name was changed to Bousfield in 1913, after Sir William Bousfield, a former chairman of the managers. The old school building is now occupied by Our Lady of Victories Primary School.

Trevor Bowen

When John Barker died in 1914, 34-year-old Trevor Bowen (c.1880-1965) was appointed manager of **Barker's** food section. Bowen, who was born in Monmouthshire, had been manager of Lyons Bakery near Olympia at Cadby Hall. In August 1914, he was involved in the gigantic task of army catering – carried out by private contractors before the establishment of the Catering Corps. One of his first big contracts was the feeding of 'Kitchener's Army' waiting in depots to go overseas.

The new chairman of Barker's was Sydney Skinner and together they negotiated the merger with **Derry and Toms.** However it was their ambitious expansionist plans, including into **Kensington Square** that was to cause controversy. A seventy year battle ensued with the Council and local residents, in particular those living in Kensington Square who objected to the 'Barkerisation' of their neighbourhood and amenities. Worn down by the fighting Skinner became seriously ill in 1940 and Trevor Bowen took over as Chairman. Finally the rebuild-

26. Trevor Bowen, expansionist chairman of Barker's, in his uniform as a Deputy Lieutenant for the County of London.

ing work got underway in 1937 but was not completed until 1958.

Following the successful bid for the store by House of Fraser in 1957, Bowen became Honorary President, a position he held until his death in 1965. He was given a handsome office in the Derry building, but he had little to do but recall past glories and reflect sadly that he was never offered a knighthood, blaming this on his clash with municipal leaders. Luckily this did not prevent him from leaving his personal archive, containing photographs, some dating back to the 1860s, ephemera and the Roof Garden visitor books, to the Borough's Local Studies Library.

Britannia Brewery

Despite its many public houses, old Kensington seems to have had only one brewery in the vicinity of the town centre. This was the Britannia, established in

27. The Britannia Brewery c.1926, just prior to demolition.

about 1834 by Edward Herrington and William Wells. This new venture, on a site in Allen Street now occupied by Allen Mansions, was ambitious. It was a purpose-built industrial block with loading loft and arched entrance to the yard and stables. Sadly the enterprise did not pay. Known later as William Wells & Co it was faced with bankruptcy in 1902, but recovered until 1924 when Young's bought it up. Only two of its outlets remain – the Britannia in Allen Street and the Britannia Tap in Warwick Road. The name came from the handsome statue on the brewery roof.

Benjamin Britten

Britten's mother provided his earliest musical inspiration. A keen singer, Britten (1913-1976) was the accompanist and composer at her musical soirées. Schooled at South Lodge preparatory school he earned a scholarship to the Royal College of Music. Here he was taught by Frank Bridge and John Ireland. His lifelong partner, both romantically and musically, was singer Peter Pears whom he met in 1927.

Working as composer for the General Post Office Film Unit he wrote for radio, theatre and cinema. Here he collaborated with

28. *Benjamin Britten (right) and the composer, Lennox Berkeley. Photograph by Howard Coster, 1938. © National Portrait Gallery, London*

Brompton

During the 17th and 18th centuries the village of Brompton was renowned for its wholesome, clean air, flourishing markets and nurseries. The most famous, run by the celebrated gardeners London and Wise, was **Brompton Park Nursery**, where the **Victoria & Albert Museum** now stands.

The early 19th century saw a huge change in London's landscape. An increase in building developments led to the transformation of Brompton from a prosperous rural parish to a busy metropolitan area. The first developments took place between 1760 and 1770, when terraced houses with large front gardens were built along the present day Brompton Road. This part of the road was named 'New Brompton' to distinguish it from the original village further west, which became 'Old Brompton'.

Further building took place during the 1820s boom and by the 1830s Brompton Road was a prosperous residential area. In the second half of the 19th century the south side of Brompton Road was transformed into a fashionable shopping street. The old terraced houses were pulled down to be replaced by shops to attract the tourists flocking to the area to visit the new museums.

The residential blocks at the south-west end of Brompton Road were constructed between 1886 and 1890. The Bell and Horns Inn was demolished to make way for Empire House, Dalmeny House and the Rembrandt Hotel buildings which were built between 1910 and 1927.

W H Auden on various documentaries, then later on *Our Hunting Fathers* and *On This Island*. He also wrote many orchestral pieces. Travelling to North America in 1939 inspired his first large-scale instrumental pieces and vocal music for Pears. Returning to England he wrote *Peter Grimes*, performed in 1945, the first opera written by an Englishman since Purcell. Other famous operas include *Billy Budd*, *Gloriana* and *The Turn of The Screw*.

Cromwell Road was Britten's home during his university days where he composed copiously, including *Sinfonietta* and *A Boy Was Born*. He could never shake off the feeling that he was not valued and certainly some viewed his work as being "too clever by half".

Broadwood family

Best known for their piano making business in St James's, the Broadwood family also owned land in Kensington. In 1803 the family inherited land surrounding an ancient footpath known as Love Lane. Thomas and John Broadwood enlisted the help of the architect Thomas Cundy III in laying out a small estate here in the 1860s. Cundy designed two parallel roads with houses facing each other across a central ornamental garden. Originally the development was to be called Gloucester Gardens, but this was changed to **Cornwall Gardens.**

Thomas Broadwood died in 1881 and the estate passed to his nephew Walter George King. Following his death in 1905 the freeholds were gradually sold.

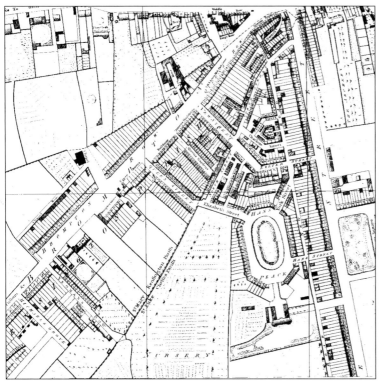

29. *The Brompton area in Horwood's map of the early 19th century, showing the almost rural nature of the surroundings.*

colonnades. Names on headstones include Mr Nutkin, Mr McGregor, Tod, Jeremiah Fisher, Tommy Brock – and even a Peter Rabbett.

On 13 June 1892, the American Sioux Indian Chief, Long Wolf, was buried here. He died aged 59 of bronchial pneumonia whilst touring Europe with Buffalo Bill's Wild West Show. Due to the efforts of housewife Elizabeth Knight in 1997, Chief Long Wolf was finally moved to a new plot in the Wolf Creek Community Cemetery at Pine Ridge, South Dakota, to rejoin his people in their happy hunting grounds.

The cemetery is a haven for wildlife including birds, butterflies, foxes and squirrels and is managed by the Royal Parks. Each year the London Wildlife Trust arranges a number of guided walks covering different aspects of Brompton's flora and fauna.

Brompton Cemetery

Inadequate sanitary conditions led to endemic disease and increased mortality in the early part of the 19th century and the churchyard burial grounds were unable to cope. Parliament authorised, between 1832 and 1841, the establishment of seven commercial cemeteries around London, of which the West of London and Westminster Cemetery on Old Brompton Road, as Brompton Cemetery was known, is an outstanding example.

The cemetery, designed by Benjamin Baud, is regarded as one of the finest Victorian metropolitan cemeteries in the country. It has a formal layout with a central avenue leading to a chapel based on St Peter's Basilica in Rome. There are over 35,000 monuments, many of historical importance.

The gravestones found here include those for Emmeline Pankhurst, Suffragette leader; Richard Tauber, singer and operetta composer; Percy Lambert, motor racing pioneer and the first person to cover 100 miles in an hour; Dr John Snow, pioneer anaesthetist and discoverer of the cause of cholera; Sir Francis Pettit Smith, inventor of the four-bladed screw propeller; Francis Nicholson, water colourist and Alfred Mellon, violinist and music director.

Beatrix Potter, who lived nearby, took the names of many of her animal characters from tombstones in the cemetery and it is said that Mr McGregor's walled garden was based on the

Brompton Oratory

The Oratory, or to give it its full name, the Oratory of St Philip Neri and the Immaculate Heart of Mary, was built in 1882 to the designs of Herbert Gribble in the Baroque Italian style. Gribble stated that his design gave those who had no opportunity to visit Italy, a model of an Italian church in London. The interior is even more sumptuous; filled with gold, Sienna marble and Venetian mosaics, many gifts from the Continent. The general design follows that of the Gesu Church in Rome with a nave and side chapels instead of aisles. Mazzuoli's gigantic 17th-century marble statues of the Apostles were originally in Sienna Cathedral. One of the altars came from the Dominican

30. *A bird's-eye view of Brompton Cemetery, 1849.*

31. *Brompton Oratory c.1905.*

32. *The sumptuous interior of the Brompton Oratory c.1896.*

church in Brescia and another from St Servatius at Maastricht. The High Altar has paintings of the life of St Philip Neri.

Until Westminster Cathedral opened in 1903 it was London's premier Catholic Church. Cardinal Newman's monument, detailed in the Italian Style, stands a little west of the Oratory.

Brompton Park Nursery

In 1681, George London (d.1714) and three other eminent head gardeners established the Brompton Park Nursery and in 1687, when the other three partners had died or retired, George London took Henry Wise (1653-1738), a former apprentice, into partnership. Under London and Wise, Brompton Park became the foremost nursery in the land.

33. *Brompton Park House, former home of Henry Wise, with the International Exhibition building of 1862 in the background.*

Both drew their inspiration from France and Holland, favouring avenues and topiary. They played a major part in the construction of most of the great formal gardens of the period, including Chelsea Hospital, Longleat, Chatsworth, Melbourne Hall and Castle Howard. Wise was appointed Royal Gardener to Queen Anne and George I and was responsible for the laying out of **Kensington Gardens**.

Wise's home was Brompton Park House, where he brought up a family of ten children. This became part of South Kensington Museum until it was demolished in 1899 to make way for the new **Victoria & Albert Museum** building.

Brompton Road Station

The Piccadilly Line, opened in 1906, brought a fresh wave of visitors to the area. Planned to take advantage of the nearby museum attractions, Brompton Road Station was located at 206 Brompton Road between the Oratory and Brompton Square. However, due to lack of use the station closed in 1934. It was decorated by Leslie Green in his trademark ox-blood red tiles.

During the Second World War, the platforms were bricked up to be converted into offices, and floors were built in one of its three lift shafts to convert it into a four-storey operations centre for use as London's anti-aircraft control centre. Since then the Territorial Army and Ministry of Defence have used both the surface building and part of the underground complex.

Although the surface building was partially demolished in the 1960s, a small distinctive part of the façade can still be seen in a side street off the Brompton Road. Surface access to the platforms below is theoretically possible, but is prohibited, as the building, lift shafts and staircase are still owned by the Ministry of Defence. The below-ground section is owned by Transport for London.

Around Christmas 1994, a 20-year-old student was found at the bottom of the lift shaft having fallen down from the surface building. Nobody knows how he got there or what he was doing in the building. An open verdict was pronounced in the subsequent enquiry.

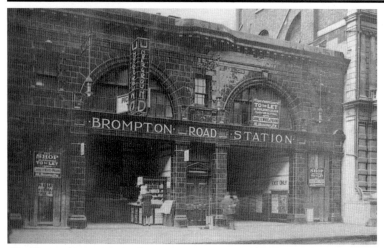

34. Situated between the Oratory and Brompton Square, the Brompton Road station was opened on the Piccadilly line in 1906. It closed in 1934.

Norman-Butler family

The Norman-Butler family can claim to have one of the lengthiest family links with Kensington as Belinda Norman-Butler's great grandfather, **William Thackeray**, was a resident from 1843. Thackeray's daughter Anne Ritchie lived in Kensington Square and was a friend of many eminent Kensington residents. She was also **Leslie Stephen's** sister-in-law. Harriet, her sister, was Stephen's first wife. **Virginia Woolf** in her novel *Night and Day* based the character of Mrs Hilbery on Anne. Belinda's mother, born at 6 Grenville Place, was the daughter of the social reformer **Charles Booth** and Mary Macaulay, niece of the historian Thomas Macaulay.

The late Edward Norman-Butler's family connections are also numerous including Montagu Norman, Governor of the Bank of England from 1920 to 1944. He lived at Thorpe Lodge, Campden Hill.

35. George Canning, from an oil painting by Thomas Gainsborough.

George Canning

Gloucester Lodge was built in 1800 on the site of the pleasure-ground **Florida Gardens** and named after its first occupant Maria, Duchess of Gloucester, sister-in-law of George III. Between 1809 and 1825 it was the residence of the Tory politician George Canning (1770-1827). Born into a poor but aristocratic family, Canning attended Eton and Oxford and became an MP in 1824. He solved his financial difficulties by marrying an heiress worth £100,000, a union which in part gave him a reputation of an ambitious adventurer. Aged 37, he became Foreign Secretary in Castlereagh's government. The two became fierce rivals, culminating in a duel during which Canning was wounded in the leg. He resigned his office but following Castlereagh's suicide in 1822, he once more became Foreign Secretary. Canning was involved with securing independence for the former Spanish colonies in South America and the Greeks from Turkish control. On the death of the Prime Minister, Lord Liverpool, he briefly became Prime Minister. Worn out by the demands of office he died in 1827.

Lord Byron paid tribute to his ability as a speaker, when he referred to him as "our last, our best, our only orator". Canning is buried in Westminster Abbey and his statue stands in Parliament Square.

Canziani Family

In 1885 Francesco Canzianni and his wife, the painter Louisa Starr, purchased 3 Palace Green, previously home to the Clerk of Works at Kensington Palace. It was here that their daughter, Estelle, grew up and was to live for the rest of her long life. She too was an artist whose pictures of birds and fairies in Kensington Gardens enjoyed several decades of popularity. Estelle signed her pictures with a star and a crescent for the C of Canziani. She also painted a series of very detailed paintings of her home, which together with family photographs give an excellent picture of their lives. Estelle was very reclusive, but was a much loved member of the Hammersmith Quakers. When she died in 1967 the house was put up for sale and later demolished to build flats.

Francesco Canzianni was an Italian engineer who after his marriage to his cousin Louisa Starr in 1882 moved to England. Here he fostered business links between England and Italy, especially in the engineering field. Motorised buses and threshing machines were two of the products he introduced into Italy.

Louisa came to London to study art at the age of fourteen and showed prodigious talent. In 1861 she became one of the first women to study at the Royal Academy Schools, a feat she achieved by applying under the name L Starr. By the time the place had been offered it was too late for them to withdraw. Most years she had a Show Sunday at Palace Green, when the studio was opened up to visitors. This was a common practice of Kensington's artist elite and took place on the Sunday before the summer Royal Academy show.

Howard Carter

Carter (1873-1939), the famous archaeologist and Egyptologist, was born and brought up at 10 Richmond Terrace (now part of the Old Brompton Road) and lived at 19 Collingham Gardens as an adult.

He served with the Egyptian Exploration Fund working mainly as an artist and later helped to reorganise the antiquities administration for the Egyptian government. Carter's successful excavations with Lord Carnarvon in the Valley of the Kings in Luxor, Egypt, include the tombs of Amenophis I,

36. Howard Carter at the Tutankhamen site.

Hatshepsut, and Thutmose IV. His greatest achievement was the discovery in 1922 of the untouched tomb of Tutankhamen. This created a media frenzy and produced some incredible items which are on display in the Cairo museum. Carnvarvon, who funded the excavation, died in 1923, leading to a suspension of work on the tomb. Other people involved in the excavation died over the years and the media made much of a 'mummy's curse' to explain this. Carter himself died in Albert Court, Kensington Gore, sixteen years later aged a conventional 65.

G K Chesterton

Poet, author and journalist, Gilbert Keith Chesterton (1874-1936) lived in 11 Warwick Gardens until his marriage when he moved to 1 Edwardes Square. In the first year there he painted crayon frescos of knights and heroes on the outside back wall.

He was born in Sheffield

37. G. K. Chesterton.

Terrace and described his childhood as sheltered and loving. His father, Edward, was a member of the well-known Kensington auctioneer and estate agents business Chesterton's. Very popular, he made many friends, but his closest companion was his brother Cecil. Educated at St Paul's, he was remembered for debating rather than academic skills. After graduating from University College he attended Slade School of Fine Art. In 1901 he married Frances Blogg at St Mary Abbots church.

The Napoleon of Notting Hill was Chesterton's first novel in which King Auberon transforms London into independent city-states and Notting Hill declares war on its neighbours. He is now best known for his Father Brown mysteries.

Chesterton died in 1936 at his home in Beaconsfield, Buckinghamshire.

Childs family

The area opposite Earl's Court station in the early 19th century was occupied by several less than salubrious enterprises including a brewery and a floor cloth factory. In 1820 Samuel Childs with his partner Charles Freeman established a wax bleaching works to serve their wax chandler's business, off Leicester Square. In the factory's final years night lights for Prices's candle factory were produced. The works closed in 1852 and Samuel Childs began to develop Child's Street and Child's Place. An average of seven people inhabited each of these small cottages, working in such professions as building, market gardens, piano-makers, the police and laundries. Their rents enabled Childs to retire to Sunbury and lead the life of a gentleman.

Today the houses in this terrace with their small front gardens are much sought after, attracting well off people including a former star Chelsea footballer. Original street furniture including lights and bollards has been retained which help to distance the street from the more garish Earl's Court Road.

Sir Winston Churchill

Son of Lord Randolph Churchill, 7th Duke of Marlborough, Churchill (1874-1965) grew up in Dublin and London. A terror at school, he argued passionately with teachers and even destroyed a headmaster's hat. His father enrolled him for army classes at Harrow after noting Churchill's brilliant leadership of his toy soldiers. He married Clementine Hozier in 1908 and had four children.

38. Winston Churchill, c.1940.

Churchill turned to politics after a successful career as soldier, war correspondent and novelist. He won his first seat as Conservative MP for Oldham in 1900 but, after leading several backbench rebellions, joined the Liberals in 1906. The Dardanelle massacre during the First World War was the low point of his cabinet career. Banished to the Colonial Office in 1921, he redrew the map of the Middle East. Rejoining the Conservatives in 1924 he opposed Indian self-rule and the appeasement of Hitler, becoming Prime Minister after Chamberlain's resignation in 1940. A brilliant war-time leader, he ensured Britain's eventual victory but lost the 1945 election.

Attracted by its privacy, he made his home at 27 and 28 Hyde Park Gate from 1945 until his death in 1965. He wrote the *History of the Second World War* here and lectured on the Communist threat. Churchill returned as Prime Minister from 1951 to 1955, launching Brit-

39. William Cobbett in later life. A portrait published in A Constitutional Reform of Parliament.

ain's nuclear weapons programme and economic restructuring.

Receiving many honours during his lifetime, he was made Freeman of the Royal Borough in 1949. He died at home in 1965, exactly 70 years after his father.

William Cobbett

The radical politician and journalist, William Cobbett (1763-1835), was well into middle age when he moved into a cottage at the rear of **Scarsdale House**, off Kensington High Street, in 1820. It was from here that he set off on his famous 'Rural Rides'.

He served in the Army in his young days, including a spell in Canada. Shocked by Army corruption, he moved to revolutionary France and from there to America. There, he published a pro-British newspaper called *Porcupine's Gazette*, and became involved in an expensive libel action. Cobbett returned to England in 1800 and began his famous *Political Register* which ran from 1802 until his death.

Once again in trouble with the authorities he was sent to prison. On his release he took up farming, this time in America returning to England in 1817.

In Kensington Cobbett ran a small farm with cows, pigs and an abundant fruit garden. He also established a seed farm, specialising in American imports such as maize, and tree saplings. In an outbuilding he continued to print *The Political Register* and write about the people and places he encountered during his excursions around England. Cobbett left Kensington when he became an MP in 1831.

Alma Cogan

Alma (1932-1966) with her black bouffant hair, sparkly frocks and dazzling smile – she was known as the girl with the 'laugh in her voice' – died tragically young from cancer. In the late fifties. She was a huge star, singing bouncy songs and dressing sensationally, making several dress changes during each show.

At the height of her fame and fortune, Alma still lived with her mother and sister Sandra sharing a flat at 44 Stafford Court in Kensington High Street. This became known for its all-night parties, frequented by stars such as Michael Caine, Frankie Vaughan, Tommy Steele, Danny Kaye, Ethel Merman, Sammy Davis Junior and Cary Grant.

Her professional singing career began while she was still a teenager, singing songs for evening diners at the Cumberland Hotel. She began recording in 1952 with *To Be Worthy of You*. Her first chart success came in 1954 with *Bell Bottom Blues*, which got to No. 5 on the British charts. She also

40. *Sir Henry Cole, mastermind of the 1851 Exhibition and altogether a man of many achievements.*

became a close friend of the Beatles, especially John, and Brian Epstein. Alma, with their approval, covered several Lennon and McCartney songs, including *Eight Days A Week*, *Help*, *Yesterday*, *I Feel Fine* and *Ticket To Ride*.

Sir Henry Cole

Although best known as organiser of the **Great Exhibition** and first director of the **Victoria and Albert Museum**, Henry Cole (1808-1882) was a multi-talented man with an impressive list of achievements to his name. He was one of the first people to recognize the importance of combining art and industry and bringing the benefits to the masses through education and exhibitions, ideas shared by

Prince Albert, Queen Victoria's husband.

His career began at the Public Record Office where he was instrumental in reforming the organisation and the preservation of the national archive. He then worked with Rowland Hill, playing a key role in the introduction of the Penny Post. Some even credit Cole with designing the world's first postage stamp, the Penny Black. In 1843 he commissioned his friend John Calcott Horsley to design and print the first commercial Christmas card. In 1848 he created a national system of art education. Under the pseudonym Felix Summerly, he designed several items which went into production and wrote a series of children's books.

Cole's personal life was

equally rich. Married to Marian Bond in 1833 they had eight children whom he adored. His diaries are filled with his concern that all of them, both boys and girls, should get the best education and employment available, an example of his radical politics. He also had many friends whom he entertained lavishly in his house in Thurloe Place, immediately opposite the museum. He also loved dogs and was always accompanied in the museum by his favourite, Jim, who is buried in the John Madejski garden and marked by a small memorial close to the main door to the garden.

On his retirement in 1873, Cole moved to Philbeach Gardens. He was obsessed with sewers and sanitation and searched for a house which "must have a guarantee against escape of sewer gas". He found Philbeach Gardens, built by his friend George Mineard, "well planned and convenient" and loved the communal garden. Together they founded the Fifth of November Club to organise an annual firework display as well as being involved with tree planting and the provision of electric light. He died there in 1882 and is buried in Brompton Cemetery.

Coleherne Court

Coleherne Court is on the site of Coleherne House, rural retreat of poet-physician Sir Richard Blackmore. The name Coleherne dates back to 1430.

Without doubt the most famous recent occupant of the Court was **Diana, Princess of Wales**. Her father, the Earl Spencer, gave Diana the flat as an 18th birthday present. She

41. Stewart Granger.

moved in with three girlfriends in July 1979. On her bedroom door there was a sign 'Chief Chick'. On 23 February 1981 she moved into Clarence House, the next day her engagement to Prince Charles was announced.

Other recent residents include another royal bride, Sophie Rhys-Jones, Countess of Wessex and the novelist Brigid Brophy (1929-95) who lived here in the 1950s. Meetings of the Workers' Revolutionary Party were regularly held in flat 116, when occupied by the actor Corin Redgrave and his family. An earlier resident, Princess Mestchersky, leader of White Russian exiles, would have been very disturbed.

In May 1913 James Leblanche Stewart was born in flat 60 and most of his childhood was spent here. Obliged to change his acting name to avoid confusion with the American film star, he is known better as Stewart Granger (1913-1993). Following a very successful career on the English stage, he moved to America and went on to star in several Hollywood films.

The College of Psychic Studies

Spiritualists believe that the human personality survives bodily death and that this fact is capable of demonstration.

The London Spiritualist Alliance was founded in 1883, but it was not until 1925 that the Alliance was able to acquire premises of its own. The purchase price was £5,000 for the freehold of 16 Queensberry Place. Funds were donated by those who were bereaved during the First World War, but had gained solace through spiritualism. Sir Arthur Conan Doyle, an avid supporter of spiritualism, was President in the 1920s. The college encourages the work of mediums and today operates as an educational charity offering both courses and consultations. The present name was adopted in 1970.

Comedians

Despite a lack of theatres and music halls, the area has since the 1820s been very popular with entertainers. Comic actors such as William Farrin and John Lister, have long since been forgotten but recent residents include the very best comedians of the age, three honoured with plaques on their homes.

Benny Hill (1924-1992) lived at 1-2 Queen's Gate from 1960 until 1986 when he was forced out by building work. The video for his hit single *Ernie, the Fastest Milkman in the West* was filmed in Queen's Gate Mews. Famous for his 'postcard humour' he was either loved or loathed. When the *Benny Hill Show* was axed many thought that would be the end of his career but he went on to enjoy many years of international success, especially in America. For over forty years Benny was one of Britain's best known and loved comedians.

The Dead Comic Society plaque in honour of Frankie Howerd (1917-1992) was unveiled by Cilla Black outside 27 Edwardes Square, his home from 1966 to 1996. It was accompanied by a sale of Frankie memorabilia. His career spanned six decades but is perhaps best known for his *Up Pompeii!* series. Many thought he adlibbed his famous off-the-cuff asides, in reality they were well rehearsed, often while pacing in the garden square.

Comedienne Hattie Jacques (1924-1980), well-loved stalwart of fourteen *Carry On* films, served as a factory worker and a nurse during the Second World War. She made her stage debut at the age of twenty and her first film two years later. By then she had moved into 65 Eardley Crescent, where she was to live for the rest of her life. Her television partnership with Eric Sykes lasted from 1959 until her death. In June 1995 her enormous contribution was honoured when the first Comic Heritage plaque for an actress was unveiled by Eric Sykes at her home.

John le Mesurier (1912-1983) met Hattie in 1946 and shortly after moved into Eardley Crescent. They were married in 1952 and divorced in 1965 but they remained good friends. John had a long and distinguished career but is best known for his portrayal of Sergeant Wilson in *Dad's Army*.

The Dead Comics Society has also honoured another *Carry On* star, Joan Sims, who lived in Esmond Court.

Actor, cartoonist and TV panellist, Willie Rushton (1937-1996) was born in 1937 at 28 Scarsdale Villas and 24 years later this was to be the birthplace of *Private Eye*. He met the other founders of the magazine while at Shrewsbury school. The first issue of *Private Eye* appeared on 25 October 1961, having been put together in Rushton's bedroom using Letraset and Cow Gum. The Profumo scandal first broke in the magazine when Stephen Ward confessed all to Rushton.

Willie died at the Cromwell Hospital in 1996 from complications after a heart operation.

Comedian Derek Nimmo (1930-1999) lived in Earl's Court with his wife Patricia for over 30 years. It was at his home that he had a serious fall, fell into a coma and died shortly after in Chelsea and Westminster Hospital. Although he appeared in several films and plays he is best known for his radio and television appearances. He was a regular panellist on *Just a Minute,* between 1963 and 1986 and appeared in several British sitcoms and comedy series, often as a cleric, including *All Gas and Gaiters*, *Oh Brother, Oh Father* and *Life begins at 40.*

Commonwealth Institute

The distinctive Commonwealth Institute building with its hyperbolic copper roof has been a feature of Kensington High Street since the late 1950s but today it is threatened with demolition.

The Institute's predecessor was the Imperial Institute, established in South Kensington in 1888 – its tower remains and is now part of Imperial College. This had been set up by the Government as an educational and research centre, assisting and promoting commercial and scientific activities in Britain and the colonies. In 1962 it moved to Kensington High Street.

Times had changed in Britain's relationship with her former colonies and a Commonwealth of Nations replaced the former

42. *The Commonwealth Institute shortly after opening in 1962.*

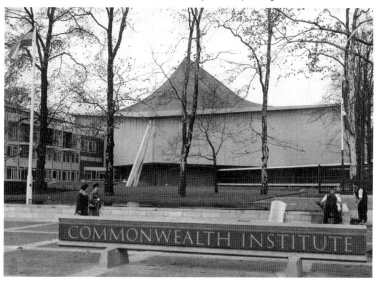

Empire. These former colonies, linked by shared histories, now met as equals under the guiding principles of co-operation and mutual support. It was time for a new building with a modern outlook.

The building, developed between 1958 and 1962, was designed by Sir Robert Matthew of Johnson, Marshall and Partners, who had also designed the Royal Festival Hall. The building's open-plan interior, which provided gallery space for all Commonwealth countries, was designed by James Gardner. The gardens, water features and grounds were the work of landscape architect Dame Sylvia Crowe. The building is listed Grade II* and has been described by English Heritage as "the most important public building of architectural ambition raised in London between the time of the Royal Festival Hall and the Hayward Gallery."

However there is now an application to de-list it and pave the way for redevelopment. This situation was brought about when the functions of the Institute were moved from Kensington and the building vacated.

Convent of the Assumption

The Order was founded in Paris by Blessed Marie Eugenie in 1839, who is expected to be canonised in 2006. The focus of their mission was working with young people and educational projects. Today it boasts of 1300 members working in thirty-five countries.

The nuns first took up residence at Earl's Court Lodge but unable to purchase the site they acquired a block of houses in

43. An 1873 drawing of the apse of the Convent of the Assumption

Kensington Square. At first they occupied 23-24 Kensington Square where the nuns kept cows and chickens in a large garden at the rear. The sisters went on to build a chapel, a primary school and a large educational block, all designed in the Gothic style by George Goldie. The chapel was seriously damaged in a fire in 1957 and has been reconstructed in a less ornate manner with a blue concrete roof over the nave. More recently a student hostel and a new convent have been added.

Number 20 was let out until 1892 when it was used as a boys' prep. school. A block was built in the garden and utilised for training girls for domestic service; it later became St Catherine's finishing school. During the War the schools were evacuated and never returned. Instead the education block was taken over by a Catholic teacher training foundation, Marie Assumpta College from 1946 to 1978.

Today, the convent is a centre for various Christian educational and pastoral organisations. The garden, although much

reduced, is filled with plane, oak and mulberry trees and is occasionally open to the general public.

Corbett & McClymont

The main force behind development in the south part of the **Gunter Estate** was the partnership of William Corbett and Alexander McClymont. From 1864 to 1878, they constructed the 'Redcliffe Estate' sited between the Brompton and Fulham Roads.

The story of the rise and fall of these two men is a sad one, and mirrors the fate of so many Georgian and Victorian builder speculators. Although they built more houses, some 750, in southern Kensington than any other builder, in 1878 they went bankrupt owing £1.25 million. Overextended, they were caught with too many empty houses because of a depression in the house market. In any event, they were trying to sell slightly out-of-date large houses in Redcliffe Square, whereas people now wanted smaller red brick houses.

William Corbett began his career as a clerical worker in the solicitors' office of Messrs Lewins of Southampton Row. This connection was useful to him when he went into building work. Lewins not only did Corbett and McClymont's legal work, but also provided some of the building finance. Alexander McClymont was a bank manager. At some point in the 1850s the two men formed a building company with McClymont dealing with the day-to-day building business and Corbett with the financial and legal side.

Cornwall Gardens

Cornwall Gardens on the **Broadwood estate** is an interesting and innovative example of the Italianate style, designed by Thomas Cundy III. The Broadwoods, owners of the celebrated piano making business in St James's, used some of their profits to purchase a small plot in Kensington. In 1862 they employed Cundy to design the layout. This comprised of two parallel rows of Italianate stucco houses facing onto an ornamental garden. Other special features included three water closets, white faced brick and Portland cement and cast iron railings, which sadly were lost to the Second World War salvage drive. William Willett was responsible for building many of the houses including the rather exuberant Garden House and Cornwall House *(ill. 45)*.

The Gardens were named in honour of the 21st birthday of the Prince of Wales, Duke of Cornwall in November 1862. However, it was more frequently called Mayne's Village Community because of the large number of old India hands residing there including Sir Henry Mayne, a North Indian administrator and author. The central garden boasts some of the tallest and oldest plane trees in London. Planted in 1870 they help to create the atmosphere of a woodland garden in the centre of London. Famous residents include the artist **Sir Joseph Boehm** (no. 78), author Ivy Compton Burnett and **Terence Rattigan**.

44. Marie Corelli.

Marie Corelli

Marie Corelli (1855-1924) was the most popular novelist in the late 19th century, outselling Hall Caine, Mrs Humphry Ward, H G Wells, and Arthur Conan Doyle by the thousands. Mary Mackay began her career as a musician, adopting the stage name Marie Corelli. She gave up music and turned to writing instead. In 1886 her first novel *A Romance of Two Worlds* was published. She was a prolific writer but her works are now largely forgotten.

One of her chief admirers was the Prime Minister, William Gladstone. A resident of Longridge Road, The Rev. Dugald MacColl, Minister of the nearby Kensington Presbyterian Church, tells of the day "when Mrs Gladstone was left in her carriage outside no. 47 to enjoy the fresh air for two solid hours and more while her wonderful spouse and the younger leader of religious thought conferred ... surely a tablet should mark the spot."

Marie lived at Longridge Road with her life long companion Bertha Vyer and her pet dog.

45. *Cornwall House (left) and Garden House c.1880.*

Counter's Creek

Counter's Creek is a small stream that rises in Kensal Green, flows through Olympia, Earl's Court and then empties into the River Thames. It formed the western boundary and in medieval times it was known as Billingwell Dyche. It is thought that Matilda, Countess of Oxford and owner of the manor built a bridge over it called 'Contessbrugge' (now Addison Bridge on the Kensington Road), hence the name Counter's Creek. It was here that Joseph Addison, who lived beside it, wrote of the larks and nightingales singing there.

All was to change when William Edwardes, 2nd Lord Kensington decided to turn it into a canal. The Kensington Canal venture was beset by disaster, as was the short lived 'Mr Punch's railway' which followed, partly on the same route. It was only with the arrival of the West London Extension Railway that a viable transport network was achieved, and recently, with new housing developments along the line of the old Counter's Creek, the West Brompton railway station has been reopened. Following the cholera outbreak of 1848-9 the old stream was filled in as a health hazard.

Col. Rookes Evelyn Bell Crompton

Kensington Court had a reputation for modern amenities, which resulted in an increased demand for electric lighting. This inspired Colonel R E B Crompton (1845-1940), a pioneer of electrical engineering, to convert an old shed into a generating station. A dynamo transmitted direct current on bare copper mains through subways to the houses to charge batteries or accumulators. This system quickly expanded to become the Kensington and Knightsbridge Electric Lighting Company in a basement below street level that remained as a sub-station until 1985. The old hydraulic power station has been converted into private accommodation at the opposite end of Thackeray Street.

Crompton lived with his wife Elizabeth and five children at 48 Kensington Court, where he also had a laboratory. Supporting standardisation he established the National Physical Laboratory, now called the British Standards Institution. Passionately interested in cars, he founded the RAC in 1896, judged the first motor show in 1903 and sat on the government road board in 1910.

Cromwell Road

Cromwell Road is one of the Borough's major thoroughfares and is designated part of the A4. It took over a century to create it. Although named after Oliver Cromwell it is doubtful that he had any association with Kensington. However, his son Henry was married at **St Mary Abbots Church** and is thought to have stayed at Hale House, sited near the present junction of Queen's Gate and Cromwell Road.

The first section of the road, between Thurloe Place and Gloucester Road, was built in the 1850s by the 1851 Commissioners to service their new estate purchased with the profits from the **Great Exhibition**. Fol-

46. Cromwell Road c.1905.

lowing the success of this enterprise three landowners, the **Alexanders**, the **Gunters**, and Lord Kensington, worked together to extend the road to Earl's Court. Lord Kensington, meanwhile, was also building the section to the Warwick Road which when opened in 1876 was called West Cromwell Road. The effect was to immediately open up the area and housing development gathered apace.

For a further seventy years the road ended at the West London Extension Railway. Anyone travelling further west had to turn down Warwick Road and cross via Addison Bridge on Kensington High Street. Similar problems were encountered on the Talgarth Road, the other side of the railway. It was not until 1941 that the West Cromwell Road Bridge was built linking the two roads. The project was completed with the building of the Hammersmith flyover and widening of the West Cromwell Road in 1972.

The fine houses lining the road, especially in the western sections, quickly became divided into flats and lodging houses, many looking much the worse

for wear. New multi-storey concrete and glass hotels sprang up in the 1970s round the Gloucester Road intersection. In one section, backing on to Stanhope Gardens, eleven listed properties in a tragic state of disrepair, were restored and in 2003 converted into serviced apartments.

William Henry Davison (1st Lord Broughshane)

Sir William Davison (1872-1953), Mayor of Kensington during the First World War, offered to raise and equip an extra battalion by recruiting civilian volunteers from local shops and offices. They were to become C and D companies of the 22nd Battalion of the Royal Fusiliers, better known as the Kensington's. He not only recruited the troops, but also supplied their uniforms made of khaki from Harrods at a cost £1. 7s. 0d., shirts from Derry and Toms and 1000 Kropp razors. Davison also made arrangements for the training camp at Horsham including all domestic necessities from beds to cutlery. In July 1915, this

largely citizen's army of nearly 1000 men, now equipped and trained, was handed over to the War Office and left for France in November.

Sadly, few of the men parading so proudly outside the Town Hall were to return as most were slain on the fields of Flanders. In May 1917 their Commander, Col. Barnett Barker wrote to Davison: "The regiment doesn't exist ... only 40 men returned with me. They fought and died as heroes ... I am sick of bloody battles and everything connected with them". Davison was informed of each casualty and wrote personally to their next of kin.

In 1918, Davison was elected Mayor for the fifth time and knighted for his war services. He became MP for Kensington, South Division from 1918 to 1945, when he was elevated to the peerage and became Lord Broughshane. The title came from the family estate in Ulster near the Antrim coast. His youngest son, born in 1914, was christened William Kensington. Throughout his long service to Kensington, Davison compiled personal scrapbooks which were donated to the Local Studies Library. They contain a wealth of fascinating material and photographs, including samples of Khaki from Harrods.

Day Estate

The Day Estate, situated north of the Old Brompton Road, was owned by the Dyson family from 1661. When a member of the family defaulted on a loan it was acquired by Walter Dodemead, who left it to his three daughters. James Day inherited the land from his aunt in 1772.

The land, originally known as the 'Six Acres' although it is just under ten acres, is now occupied by Hereford Square, Brechin Place, Rosary Gardens and Wetherby Place. The estate also included a three-acre field to the south of the Old Brompton Road, now the northern end of Drayton Gardens.

By the 1830s, residences known as Brompton Villa, Clareville, **Hereford Lodge** and the Rosary were ranged along the Old Brompton Road, with a farmyard, pleasure ground, paddocks and gardens to their north. **Hereford Square** was begun in 1845 and **Drayton Gardens** shortly after. Building was not completed until 1885. The houses were popular with the genteel classes, especially annuitants and retirees, and were of a very high quality. Prospectuses boasted of hot and cold water, several bathrooms, billiard rooms, libraries and separate wine cellars. To maintain the tone, residents were banned from conducting businesses except those associated with medicine and the arts. Schools for young ladies were also allowed. Famous residents include the writer George Borrow and actress **Fanny Kemble** in Hereford Gardens, actor-manager **Beerbohm Tree** at 31 Rosary Gardens and Anne Thackeray at 5 Wetherby Place.

De Vere Gardens

De Vere Gardens was built on the site of Grimwood's Kensington Nursery. These were exceptionally large grand buildings: nos. 28 and 30 had eighteen bedrooms each. Early residents often employed distinguished artists, such as Halsey Ricardo and Walter Stokes, to embellish their already opulent homes. However, the tide was beginning to turn against such houses and they were slow to sell.

Matters were not helped by the dispute over the site of what is now the De Vere Hotel. Residents expecting a grand corner house were confronted by what they described as 'three barns'. The case went all the way to the House of Lords, by which time the developer had gone bankrupt. In the 1880s most of the large houses became flats or hotels, either by conversion or purpose-built. In 1897 the 'barns' were remodelled as the De Vere Hotel, with an iron and glass porch designed by Walter Groves and winged lions by Alfred Drury.

Famous residents include writers Robert Browning and Henry James, the Marquess of Carmarthen and John Heaton MP, Commissioner for New South Wales.

Derry & Toms

James Toms was the first of the significant names to appear on the High Street. He opened a grocery store just east of Young Street in 1824. A few doors away, on the site of the present station entrance, Joseph Toms, possibly James's son, opened a toy and fancy goods store in 1836. His sister Christiana married Charles Derry, a draper, who had a store on the corner of Wright's Lane and so Derry & Toms was born. The commercial partnership was formalized in 1869 and they purchased nos. 107-111 Kensington High Street. Development was rapid and expansion gathered apace till by 1900 they owned all the proper-ties from Derry Street to the railway plus properties behind the High Street. But business slumped during the Great War and in January 1920 they merged with **Barker's**.

Architect Bernard George was commissioned to produce designs for both Barker's and Derry & Toms. The new Derry & Toms store was opened in March 1933, amidst a fanfare of press publicity, "a beautiful store to sell beautiful things". Arranged on six floors it was a bold departure in store design, with a stone façade of columns and friezes and marble and bronze Art-Deco panels providing the only decorative features inside. Derry & Toms was one of the first London stores to adopt the horizontal system, whereby each floor was totally open plan thus reducing the fire risk. On the fifth floor there was an elegant restaurant, The Rainbow Room, and a fashion theatre. Finally in 1938 the **Roof Garden** was opened. Contemporaries described the building as having "spirit and sparkle".

Derry & Toms closed in January 1973 and the site passed to British Land and Dorothy Perkins. For a short while the days of glory returned when **Biba** opened there in 1973, sadly to close two years later. Since then the site has been occupied by chain stores.

47. *The Derry & Toms building, from a watercolour by Joseph Pike.*

Drayton Gardens

The southern part of Drayton Gardens is more varied than that of the northern section on the **Day Estate**. Characterised by large mansion blocks, some of the smaller developments by individual freeholders remain. Early residents include John Burke, founder of the *Peerage*, the writer Douglas Jerrold, the artist William Cowen and the Australian explorer, Captain Mitchell. In addition to the flats put up at the turn of the century Onslow Court and Donovan Court were built in 1933-5. The latter was the home of the molecular scientist **Rosalind Franklin**.

At one time there were two cinemas, the old ABC and the Paris Pullman. Now only the ABC, today Cineworld, at the junction with Fulham Road remains. Built and opened in 1930 as the Forum Cinema it was one in a chain owned by H A Yapp. The Paris Pullman in the 1970s and early 1980s was the place to see 'art' movies especially from France and early American science fiction movies. It was opened as the Radium Picture Playhouse in 1911, on a site previously used as gym and dancing school. The Pullman closed in the early 1980s and together with Tiny Garage was demolished and replaced by a block of flats. There are regular reports in the local papers that a similar fate awaits the old ABC, but to date all redevelopment plans have failed.

Diana, Princess of Wales

Diana Princess of Wales (b. 1961) died on Sunday, 31 August 1997 in Paris. There was widespread mourning following her death and she is still an iconic figure today. The youngest daughter of Edward Spencer, Viscount Althorp, and his first wife, Frances Spencer, she married Prince Charles in 1981 and divorced in 1996.

She attended finishing school in Switzerland and on her return moved into an apartment in **Colcherne Court** with three friends. Whilst there she worked as a nanny, a cook and finally as an assistant at the *Young England* kindergarten in Pimlico.

In 1981 apartments 8 and 9 of **Kensington Palace** were combined to create the London residence of the newly married Prince and Princess of Wales, and it remained her official residence following their divorce. Diana and the Princes William and Harry were frequently seen in Kensington going to school, at the local MacDonald's or playing in **Kensington Gardens**.

Few will forget the amazing scenes that took place outside Kensington Palace in the days following Diana's death as the mountains of flowers, candles, teddy bears, balloons and messages grew.

Two memorials to the Princess have been sited in Kensington Gardens, a children's playground complete with a pirate boat and the jinxed Diana, Princess of Wales Memorial Fountain near the Serpentine.

Earl's Court

Between Kensington and Chelsea lies Earl's Court which derived its name from the courthouse of the Earls of Warwick and Holland, formerly Lords of the Manor.

Most of the land west of Earl's Court Lane was owned by the **Edwardes family** and almost all of it was let out as a farm. On the east side of the lane there was a small hamlet, today known as Earl's Court Village, and from the 18th century several large mansions with large grounds were built along the eastern side. It was essentially a very rural picture.

All this was to change with the advent of the railway in the mid 1860s. Normally railways were built to serve an existing population but in Earl's Court, tracks passed through agricultural land and the 'District' was for some time virtually without traffic. Here the railway acted as a stimulus to building and was warmly welcomed by landowners. Parish maps show that the area was almost totally built over between 1865 and 1879, a mere fourteen years.

Unfortunately speculative builders continued to erect large stuccoed Italianate houses designed for families with servants but by now the demand for these had fallen away. By the end of the 19th century, when large mansion blocks and brick and terracotta houses had become the norm, many of the stuccoed houses lay unsold while others were converted into flats, small hotels and hostels, a trend that was to accelerate.

One piece of empty land between the railway tracks was purchased by John Whitley who built the first **Earl's Court**

48. Harman's, cowkeeper and dairyman at 35 Earl's Court Road, c.1906. 'Families waited upon for orders. Special cows kept for the nursery and invalids'.

Exhibition ground in 1887. This was replaced in 1937 by the present Exhibition Centre

After the Second World War regeneration was slow compared to other areas. The abundance of cheap accommodation and its convenient location made the area popular with students and the young. Polish refugees were the first to arrive followed in the 1950s by students from South Africa, Rhodesia and Australia. Arrivals in the 1970s included Arabs, Iranians and Filipinos. This has all contributed to making Earl's Court a lively and cosmopolitan area.

49. Earl's Court Farm in the 1860s. The old manor house is in the background.

Earl's Court Farm

Looking around bustling Earl's Court today it is hard to imagine that 130 years ago most of the area was farmland. Earl's Court Farm spread over some 190 acres and was tenanted by generations of the Hutchins family who used it for mixed arable and market gardening. Samuel Hutchins was a noted friend of the poor, employing many as casual labourers on the farm. After his death in 1844 most of the land on the western side of Earl's Court Road was let to Samuel Allaway, a market gardener. The farm buildings were demolished and the land sold between 1875 and 1878. The old farmhouse used to stand where Earl's Court station is today.

Earl's Court Exhibition Centre

A triangle of waste ground between the railway tracks was described by its purchaser, John Whitley as nothing but "a cabbage-field and a sea-kale swamp". From such inauspicious beginnings grew one of the most popular and successful places of entertainment in London.

During a visit to Washington, Whitley witnessed a parade by Col. William Cody and his Rough Riders and determined to bring the show to England. In 1887 the exhibition opened at Earl's Court and with the Rocky Mountains as a backdrop, Buffalo Bill's troupe included 110 Indians and their families, 150 cowboys, 8 steers, 16 buffaloes, the Deadwood stagecoach and Annie Oakley. They performed in front of 15,000 visitors every day for five months, including the Queen and Mr. Gladstone. The equally successful Italian, French and German exhibitions followed. Unfortunately, Whitley failed to make a single penny from his efforts.

It was **Imre Kiralfy**, a Hungarian showman, who presided over the heyday of the grounds. He rebuilt the site and opened in 1894 with a spectacular Empire of India exhibition which included an Indian village imported from Poona, 200 native craftsmen, a herd of elephants from Burma and a jungle of stuffed animals. Other spectaculars followed and in

50. *A panoramic view of the Exhibition Centre at the time of the American Exhibition, 1887.*

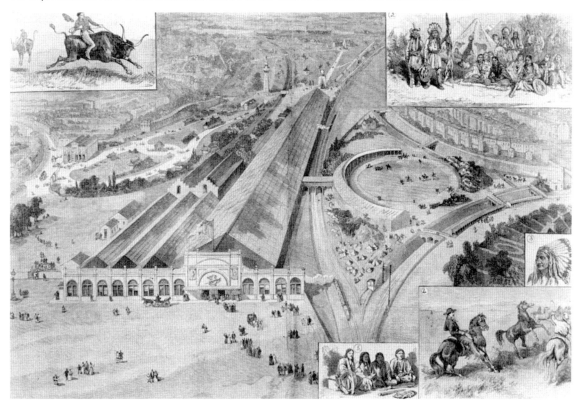

1895 the **Great Wheel** was erected.

In 1914 the last exhibition was held and the site used as a Belgian refugee camp, said to be the largest clearing house in England for dealing with the refugee problem. It then fell into total disrepair.

In 1935 the lease was granted to Earl's Court Ltd who decided to construct a show centre to rival any other in the world. The present building of reinforced concrete was constructed in 1936-7 and designed by the American architect C Howard Crane. It provided 450,000 square feet of space unimpeded by columns. It was also highly adaptable and could be used as either an auditorium overlooking an arena complete with a giant pool in the middle or flat floor exhibition space. The Ideal Home Exhibition, the Motor Show, the Boat Show, the Royal Tournament and pop concerts are just a few of the events held here. Earl's Court Two was later constructed at a cost of £100 million and opened by **Diana, Princess of Wales** on 17 October 1991. Today some two hundred events are held every year attracting over three million visitors.

Earl's Court Kangaroos

The Earls Court Kangaroos were formed as a foundation club of the British Australian Rules Football League in 1990. They changed their name to the Esher Kangaroos for the 1992 season, then to the Firkin Roos for the 1996-97 seasons, and then folded.

Their only Grand Final appearance was in 1991, when they defeated the Wandsworth Demons for the premiership.

51. *Philbeach Gardens on the Edwardes Estate, c.1905, with St Cuthbert's church in the background.*

Edwardes family and estate

The largest estate in southern Kensington, some 250 acres in extent, belonged to the Edwardes Family. On the death of the 4th Earl of Holland, who died childless, the estate passed to Elizabeth Rich, wife of Francis Edwardes of Pembrokeshire, and then to her son Edward who left the entailed estate to his brother William. In 1776 William was created a Baron and took the title Lord Kensington. He was succeeded in 1801 by his son William.

Unfortunately he was a profligate and in perpetual debt, problems he tried to solve through involvement in speculative ventures, including building. Although he did extensive damage to the family fortune, luckily for his successors, the estate was entailed and therefore he could not touch the capital. He died in 1852 in a small house on the estate with debts totalling £270,000. The 3rd Lord Kensington was marginally more successful but it was only when his son William in-

herited in 1872 that development began and fortunes improved.

In 1902 the 6th Lord Kensington sold the area south of the Pembroke Road to Edward Guinness, Baron Iveagh and the remainder in smaller blocks the following year. Since then ownership has been very fragmented.

The major developments on this estate were Pembroke Road and Square, Warwick Road and Gardens, the western sections of **Cromwell Road** and Old Brompton Road, Lexham Gardens, Nevern and Earl's Court Squares, Longridge Road, Eardley Crescent and Philbeach Gardens.

Edwardes Square

Leigh Hunt, who lived at no. 32 from 1840-1851, is blamed for inventing, or at least encouraging the myth that Edwardes Square was built to accommodate Napoleon's invading army. The story is that the occupying force would require small houses near Holland House, as the Hollands were Francophiles and supporters of the French Emperor.

52. Edwardes Square in the 1920s.

54. T. S Eliot. By Katherina Wilczinski.

However, plans for the Square only began in 1811, by which time all threat of invasion had passed. It was the first speculative building development undertaken by the second Baron Kensington and the builder was a French émigré, Louis Leon Changeur. The plan was to build eighty houses around a large garden square with the northern side, Earl's Terrace, fronting the High Street.

By 1813 bankruptcy proceedings were taken out and Daniel Sutton, a carpet manufacturer from Wilton, and his son rescued the project. This was to be the first of many such disasters that were to befall Lord Kensington's ventures. Slowly the Square

53. The 'Temple' in Edwardes Square.

filled up and by 1819 an Act allowed the residents to raise a rate not exceeding two shillings in the pound to maintain the Square and pay for watchmen. Strict rules, with heavy fines were issued to residents who broke the rules. The Garden was laid out in 1820 with a splendid gardener's Lodge named the Temple. A landmark court case which went up to the House of Lords in 1912 has preserved the Square from developers and it was listed by English Heritage in 2003. Famous residents include **G K Chesterton**, Goldsworthy Lowes Dickenson and **Frankie Howerd.**

Earl's Terrace underwent a dramatic transformation in the 1990s. The entire range was demolished, except the façades. Luxurious homes complete with either a swimming pool or a home cinema were built behind and a private car park below.

Famous residents over the centuries include the artist Thomas Daniell, actors Sir Ian McKellen, Peter Wyngarde and Alan Bates, writers, George du Maurier, Walter Pater, Sir Henry Newbolt and J K Rowling.

Thomas Stearns Eliot

Although T S Eliot (1888-1965) claimed to dislike Kensington, he remained in the area for many years. He lived briefly in a boarding house at 33 Courtfield Road in 1933 after separating from his first wife Vivienne, and then in Grenville Place and Emperor's Gate.

Although he wrote poetry at Harvard from 1910 his career only took off under the influence of fellow Kensington resident Ezra Pound. He wrote many poems, most famously *The Wasteland* and *Old Possum's Book of Practical Cats*, the inspiration for **Lloyd-Webber's** musical *Cats*. Besides poetry he wrote for *The Times Literary Supplement*, *Athenaeum* and *The Criterion* and worked at Lloyds Bank and Faber & Faber. After converting to Anglo-Catholicism in 1927 he wrote many religious plays, including *Murder in the Cathedral*. He won the Nobel Prize for Literature in 1948.

Eliot was active in the Borough for many years. A Kensington air raid warden during the Second World War, he moved to Kensington Court Gardens after marrying Valerie Fletcher in 1957. He was nicknamed 'His Grace' by friends Dylan Thomas and Roy Campbell due to his plays and work for **St Stephen's Church**, where his urn was allowed to rest for a month.

Embassies

Count Peter Grigorevich Chernyshev, the Russian Ambassador in London resided at Kensington House from 1746 to 1755 and must surely be the first of many diplomats to reside and work in Kensington. Foreign Missions were attracted to Kensington because of an abundance of prestigious properties, many offered initially on peppercorn rents as such houses were proving difficult to lease or sell. There are over fifty embassies in the Borough mainly concentrated in the area between Notting Hill Gate and Fulham Road. Until very recently over a third of the houses in **Kensington Palace Gardens** were occupied by Embassies.

In the 1980s Kensington residents started to be concerned about the benefits. Demonstrations, noise, problems with parking, and long queues by those seeking visas were all seen as major problems by locals. This came to a head following the Iranian Embassy siege in 1980 when 26 hostages were seized and held for six days until rescued by the SAS. The risks were further intensified when in July 1994 the Israeli Embassy at 2 Palace Green was bombed by alleged Islamic terrorists.

Erard Piano Factory

In 1850, the French firm of piano and harp-makers, S and P Erard, built a factory in Kensington on the south side of today's Pembroke Road. Established in Paris in 1780, they had a London branch in Great Marlborough Street and enjoyed a world wide reputation for workmanship.

The Kensington factory was built on much the same lines as their premises in Paris, consisting of two long four-storey buildings, with rows of small windows. There were particular precautions against fire because of the stacks of timber, varnishes, polishes and other inflammable materials. Departments were separated by thick iron doors.

The owner, Pierre Erard, died in 1855 when the Kensington factory was producing a thousand instruments every year, but the business continued under the direction of his widow. In 1859 the building was enlarged to cover four acres, and the staff increased to over three hundred.

But times were changing. In Germany cheaper instruments were being mass-produced and anyway, pianos were becoming less popular in homes which were now more often flats or maisonettes. Madame Erard died in 1889 and the works closed the following year. Manufacturing continued in France and the Great Marlborough Street showroom was rebuilt to include a concert salon named after the founder.

Most of the factory site was taken by **Barker's** who built a large depository and Warwick Mansions, but retained a small

55. Douglas Fairbanks jnr.

section of the Erard workshop. The remainder of the site was used by Kensington Vestry for their depot. Today the new Kensington and Chelsea Depot, with flats above, dominates the south side of Pembroke Road.

Douglas Fairbanks Junior

Fairbanks Junior (1909-2000) followed his famous father into the movies, despite his father's active hostility. However, Junior swashed and buckled manfully enough to establish a solid if unspectacular career in silent movies and successfully transferred to sound. Between 1934 and 1937 he made five films in Britain and fell in love with the country. During the Second World War, he served in the US Navy based in England. He made his last two films in Britain, retiring in 1951 to develop a diverse career as a writer, producer and businessman. A confirmed Anglophile and high profile figure in London society in the 1950s, Fairbanks lived in opulence at 28 The Boltons. He remained discreet about his photographically recorded relationship with the Duchess of Argyll, which has recently been verified. In his sixties and seventies he returned to the screen in glossy cameo roles.

Fenelon Place

In 1851 Henry Benjamin Kent, a retired coal merchant, together with his brother, a builder and house agent, erected some model cottages in Fenelon Place. These were a simpler version of Prince Albert's model lodging houses displayed at the **1851 Exhibition**. They were called Shaftesbury cottages after the philanthropist, Ashley Cooper, 7th Earl of Shaftesbury.

Shortly afterwards, Kent entered into an agreement with Lord Kensington to develop the whole area. In twenty years a total of 120 houses were constructed and according to the 1871 census occupied by some 1000 people, an average of eight per house.

Most were swept away by the construction of the Cromwell Road Bridge in the 1940s. Piecemeal building continued until the 1990s when development of the area became the subject of a long-running controversy with two superstores battling over its future use, while locals worried over ever escalating traffic. The victors, Tesco, now have a huge building on the site with mixed housing development. Further development plans are once again causing residents great consternation.

Rachel Ferguson

Rachel (1892-1957) lived with her mother and sister in Florence after the early death of her father. Returning to London she went to school in Kensington. When she was only 16 she became a suffragette – "I was as militant as authority allowed me to be. I wanted to go to prison but was refused on the score of age." She then went to drama school, became an actress and taught dancing. Her writing career began as a drama critic and after 1925 wrote as 'Rachel' in *Punch*. The first of her nine novels came out in 1923; her second, *The Brontes went to Woolworths* (1931), is her best-known; but the most interesting is *Alas Poor Lady* (1937), which was "fuelled by her mordant social observation".

Rachel Ferguson spent her spare time drawing caricatures, playing the piano and listening to cases in the Law Courts. For many years she lived at 2 Phillimore Terrace where she wrote several books about Kensington and entertained numerous literary friends.

Finborough Theatre

Founded in 1980 in the Earl's Court area, and located above the Finborough Arms pub, the multi-award-winning Finborough Theatre presents new British writing, UK premieres of overseas drama, particularly from the English-speaking world, music theatre and an idiosyncratic selection of unjustly neglected work from the last one hundred and fifty years. It focuses on the total theatrical experience, regularly attracting the finest emerging

directors and designers to work with award-winning actors.

Small time conman Ronald True murdered the prostitute Olive Young at 13 Finborough Road in 1922, and this event became the subject of a play by Steve Hennessy at the Theatre.

Florida Gardens

Although not as grand as Ranelagh and Vauxhall, Florida Gardens *(ill. 56)*, established in 1762, flourished as a venue "well adapted to gallantry and intrigue" for over thirty years. In 1769 Rudolf Heim, a German florist and gardener, took over the management. Part of the property was used for cultivation of flowers and fruit, especially large Grafton cherries. The other part was a pleasure garden offering a semi-rural retreat and entertainment. Attractions included music, fireworks, balloon ascents, a bowling green and displays of horsemanship. Refreshments were served in a 'long room' built to accommodate five hundred people. Heim went bankrupt in the 1790s and the land was sold and Gloucester Lodge built on the grounds. It is now Stanhope Gardens.

Captain Francis Fowke

Francis Fowke (1823-1865) was a British engineer and architect as well as a Captain in the Royal Engineers. He was responsible for the conservatory, bandstands and hall in the Royal Horticultural Gardens, and parts of the **Victoria & Albert Museum** quadrangle. In 1862 he was asked to design a building for the 1862 Exhibition. Although the event attracted as many visitors as the 1851 Exhi-

56. Florida Gardens c.1827. Stanhope Gardens is on the site. (See p.42)

57. Francis Fowke, wood engraving by an unknown artist. © National Portrait Gallery, London.

bition, it was not considered a success. Much criticism was directed at the building. It was described as the 'ugliest building in London'. It was demolished and some materials were sold to the Alexandra Palace Com-pany. The remainder was blown up by the Royal Engineers.

When a competition was held to design the new Museum of Natural History entrants were asked to submit anonymously. Ironically, Captain Fowke won the competition, and the judges were the very same people who had heaped criticism on his ex-hibition building. Unfortu-nately, poor Captain Fowke died before the work started and a new architect was ap-pointed who radically changed the design.

Before his death, Fowke had been involved in the proposed Royal Albert Hall. His sketches for the exterior were the basis of the eventual design.

Rosalind Franklin

James Watson, Francis Crick, Maurice Wilkins and Rosalind Franklin (1920-1958) provided the information that revolution-ised modern biology with their discovery of the structure of DNA. Using information sup-plied by Franklin and her knowl-edge about the X-ray structure of DNA molecules, Watson and Crick proposed that DNA was made up of a double helix.

Pioneering molecular scien-tist, Rosalind Franklin was the daughter of Ellis Franklin and Muriel Frances and was born in Chepstow Villas, Notting Hill. Despite her natural brilliance, she found university far from easy. Studying during World War II meant funding cuts and having to split her time between studying and working as a Lon-don air raid warden.

Working for the Central Gov-ernment Laboratory for Chem-istry in Paris she was intro-duced to X-ray Diffraction, which was to be central to her future discoveries. Attracted by her work, King's College in-vited her to build up their X-ray Diffraction lab to help re-search DNA. She accepted and the team's discoveries became the foundation for our understanding of DNA. Franklin left King's due to problems with fellow researcher Maurice Wilkins, joining Birkbeck College, London where she researched the tobacco mosaic and polo viruses.

Unfortunately, Franklin died before the Nobel Prize awards in 1962 and is largely not only forgotten but overlooked for her contributions. In their Nobel lectures Watson and Crick cite 98 references, none are Franklin's. Only Wilkins included her in his acknowledgements.

She was rightfully honoured for her discoveries with a blue plaque on her Donovan Court home in 1992. She died tragically early of cancer at the Royal Marsden aged 37.

Sir Charles James Freake

Freake (1814-1884) came from a poor background. His father was a coal merchant and publican from Pimlico, but Freake's skill and force of personality transformed all that. Despite being worth £718,000 at his death he remained proud of his roots and never lost his cockney accent, instead persuading his genteel wife to adopt his way of speaking.

Starting as a carpenter he soon branched into building with help from his father, developing South Eaton Place and Eaton Square. Thanks to his natural business sense and connections with surveyor and architect George Basevi he went on to be described as having "made the neighbourhood of South Kensington, raising it from a neglected suburb … to … a second Belgravia." The main force behind the development of

58. Sir Charles Freake, from Vanity Fair, March 1883.

the **Smith's Charity Estate**, his major achievements include the area around Onslow Square, 48-78 Fulham Road, **St Jude's Church**, **St Paul's Church** and **St Peter's Church**. He built the National Training School for Music at his own expense in 1874-5, and appointed his friend **Arthur Sullivan** its first Principal. This earned Freake a baronetcy in 1882.

Like so many developers he took up short residencies in many of the streets he was working on including Sydney Place, three addresses in Onslow Square and Sumner Place. He later lived at 21 Cromwell Road, and it became the social hub for Kensington. Complete with ballroom and theatre, Freake hosted guests at numerous events, including the Prince of Wales and Duke of Edinburgh.

The Free French

"France has lost a battle but it has not lost the war." From all over the world General Charles de Gaulle rallied volunteers to join the fight for the Liberation of France. *Les Forces Françaises Libres* became known in Britain as the Free French. Towards the end of 1941, 1150 men had enlisted.

Their headquarters was in Carlton Gardens in London. However, de Gaulle also established headquarters in other parts of the capital, such as at the new **French Institute**, in Queensberry Place.

French Institute

Founded in 1910 by a young Frenchwoman, Marie d'Orliac, the *institute français du Royaume-Uni* brought fashionable writers and artists to the attention of a cultured London public.

As the *institut français* expanded its activities, it became necessary to find a larger permanent base, and in March 1939 it moved into new premises in Queensberry Place, designed by the architect Patrice Bonnet, and inaugurated by President Lebrun in the presence of the Princess Royal.

After renovation in 1995, the *institut français* became the headquarters of French cultural network in the UK. It offers French language courses for all levels and lectures and seminars on subjects of current cultural and social interest. The independent cinema Ciné Lumière is open to all. There is also a multi-media library, an archive and information centre which runs exhibitions, a reading circle and occasional festivals such as *'Lire en Fête'* as well

59. *The French Institute in Queensbury Place, built in 1939.*

as a Book Fair for children and young people.

Robert Furber

Robert Furber (*c.*1674-1756), the distinguished nurseryman, established the Kensington Nursery in 1710 at what is now **De Vere Gardens**. He was a supplier of fruit trees, garden flowers and 'exotics', many of which came from Bishop Compton's magnificent stock at Fulham Palace after the Bishop's death in 1713. As a member of the Society of Gardeners, led by Philip Miller, Curator of Chelsea Physic Garden, he helped regularise the naming of new varieties and the advancement of new techniques. In 1730, he published the first horticultural trade catalogue.

Today he is best known for the beautiful sets of engravings of flowers and fruits by the Flemish artist Pieter Casteels, commissioned in 1730. Arranged as a calendar, one plate for each month of the year, the illustrations show how far plant hunters had travelled to collect specimens. These exotic plants helped to foster the nursery trade, at this time so vital to the economic growth of west London. The plates, now highly collectible, served as a catalogue of the four hundred varieties which Furber regularly supplied. Further uses were suggested by Furber in his preface "would be very useful … for Painters, Carvers, Japaners etc also for the Ladies, as patterns for Working and Painting in water-colours; or Furniture for the Closet". He also found time to serve as an overseer of the poor and a churchwarden at **St. Mary Abbots** where he is buried.

Furber was succeeded by Nathaniel Grimwood and then by William Malcolm. More is known about the appearance of the nursery at this time from a charming watercolour by an unknown artist held in the Local Studies Library *(ill.117).* A shop with a double-bowed glass frontage stood facing the Kensington Road, further evidence of the advanced marketing skills shown by the Kensington Nursery owners. The sign of the pineapple can also be seen similar to that over Grimwood's shop in Arlington Street, Piccadilly. Robert Forrest, landscape gardener was the last occupant, leaving in 1847. Owing to legal complications involving the Grimwood family the site lay sterile for the next thirty years when it was sold and the construction of **De Vere Gardens** began.

Garden Squares

Garden squares are one of the defining features of Kensington and some of the best examples can be found in its southern part. Properties with garden access are much sought after often commanding the highest prices.

By the early 19th century the term 'square' was not used literally: many of the garden developments were crescents, widened terraces, circles or semi-circles. Most of the Kensington squares were built after 1850 when the Victorian desire for privacy led to the houses opening directly on to an enclosed garden – this was strictly for residents' use only. Iron railings and densely planted shrubs along the perimeter gave further protection. The eminent Victorian garden writer and horticulturalist, John Claudius Loudon, recommended many plants which could tolerate London's heavy air pollution, such as planes, almonds and sycamore.

Forty-six Kensington squares are protected from development by the 1851 Kensington Improvement Act and the Town Gardens Protection Act of 1863. Residents pay a garden rate to help towards their maintenance.

During the Second World War, the railings of many squares were taken to be melted down and used for armaments. It would appear, sadly, that most of these

60. *The old Gas, Light & Coke Co. premises on Kensington High Street, at the junction with Young Street, 1895.*

Gas, Light & Coke Company

In 1807 gas was first used to light public streets, and five years later a charter was granted to the Imperial Gas Light & Coke Co., the oldest of the lighting companies, renamed in 1876 as the Gas Light & Coke Co. It was nationalised after the last war and then re-privatised in the 1980s.

The towering gasometers, symbols of Britain's industrial past, have mostly been demolished. However, one remnant of the company's years in Kensington remains and that is their office building on Kensington High Street at the junction with Young Street. Numbers 55-61 Kensington High Street were built as a speculation in 1893-4 and the gas company was the first lessee. It is an extraordinary building greeted in turn by admiration and horror. *The Survey of London* certainly falls in the latter group as it describes it as "an astonishing, much-mutilated pile of shops and offices ... No archi-

were thrown away unused. Many squares were neglected in the 1960s and '70s and others faced threats from developers especially to build car parks beneath the garden. Recently the Council backed by Heritage Lottery funds have restored the railings most notably in Redcliffe and Bolton Gardens and garden committees have done much work on planting and improving facilities.

tect's name has come forward for this shockingly striped and ornamented edifice ... with bumptiously large shop windows and some skittish passages of terracotta decoration". Much altered today it houses the NatWest Bank.

Ernest George and Harold Ainsworth Peto

The striking terracotta houses in Collingham Gardens and Harrington Gardens are the work of the architects George and Peto. Built between 1881 and 1888 these red brick, flamboyant houses make a striking contrast with the surrounding white stuccoed terrace houses. Individually designed in a variety of vernacular styles with elaborate façades, gables, leaded lights and tall chimneys they were well publicised in architectural journals. Reactions were mixed, some finding them "refreshing" others complained of "over extravagance" and of "studied quaintness". Some of

61. *Proposal for Nos. 35-45 (odd) Harrington Gardens, by George and Peto. From* The Builder.

62. *The garden front of 39 Harrington Gardens, designed by George and Peto, 1882-3.*

63. *John Gielgud and Martita Hunt as Hamlet and Ophelia, 1929.*

Sir John Gielgud

Sir John's autobiography *Early Stages* begins with a description of his mother sitting in the hall supervising the move into 7 Gledhow Gardens when someone suggested that "the cradle ought to be brought in first as it was obvious that it might be needed any moment", thus he concludes he learnt early how to make an entrance.

His father, Frank Gielgud was married to Kate Lewis, the amenable daughter of Arthur Lewis and Kate Terry. Theirs was a compatible marriage rather than a great romance and was in very stark contrast to the more colourful Bohemian lifestyles of the rest of the Lewis and Terry clan, many of whom they strongly disapproved of and banned from their house.

They first lived at 36 Earl's Court Square but as the family grew they needed a larger house so in 1904 they moved to Gledhow Gardens. They had a wide social circle and the means to indulge their expensive tastes. Arthur, as he was christened, was a sickly child, much in-

the houses were specially commissioned such as 39 Harrington Gardens for **W S Gilbert**.

Harold Peto (1854-1933), the eighth child of the railway entrepreneur Sir Samuel Morton Peto, was educated at Harrow before qualifying as an architect. Ernest George (1839-1922) was articled to the architect Samuel Hewitt, winning the Royal Academy gold medal in his final year when he was twenty. In 1871 they went into partnership. Theirs was a popular and successful practice, employing assistants such as Edwin Lutyens, Guy Dauber and Herbert Baker. Peto lived in both 7 and 9 Collingham Gardens between 1885 and 1892 when he left London.

In 1892 after 21 years, the partnership was dissolved, due to Peto's increasing disenchantment with London, but on the condition that he would not practise architecture in the UK for the next 15 years. He went on to develop a new career in garden and interior design. A long admirer of the Italian Renaissance, this greatly influenced his work.

George was later honoured with a knighthood and the presidency of the Royal Institute of British Architects.

64. *Gielgud at the beginning of his career in the 1920s, in* The Three Sisters, *seen here with Beatrix Thomson.*

65. *W S Gilbert, by Spy, from Vanity Fair.*

dulged and idolised by his mother. He gives a vivid description of the house, the only complaints being the cold draughts and lack of hot water. His two favourite rooms were the attic, his special area where his toy theatre was kept, and the large white drawing room used for parties and celebrations. It was here that the Terry family assembled for Christmas. "First would come Grandmother, stout and jolly then Janet, Lucy and Mabel, Mother's sisters, next Marian making a superb entrance, after lunch Fred with Julia behind in lovely clothes. All of a sudden there would be a hush as an old lady had come in finding her way from one group to another settling at last in a low chair. It was **Ellen Terry**."

John went to Westminster as a boarder but was soon back home and by 1920 had joined Lady Benson's School of Drama in a drill hall in the Cromwell Road. It was during the long run of the *Constant Nymph,* which ran from 1927 to 1928, that he finally persuaded his parents to let him leave home. From then on Kate Gielgud's boudoir was papered with photos and press cuttings of John's triumphs.

Gielgud (1904-2000) was knighted in 1953 and appointed a Companion of Honour in 1977. In 1994 the Globe Theatre in Shaftesbury Avenue was renamed Gielgud in his honour.

Sir William Schwenk Gilbert

Born and raised in Pimlico, Gilbert (1836-1911) studied at King's College. Temperamental in the extreme, he veered from amiable and charming to argumentative and tetchy in a moment.

Like many successful literary men of his day, W S Gilbert trained as a barrister. It is therefore appropriate that he enjoyed his first major triumph with *Trial by Jury* in 1875. This initiated a twenty-year collaboration with the composer **Arthur Sullivan**. By 1878 Gilbert could afford to move into 24 The Boltons.

Following the commercial success of *HMS Pinafore* he commissioned **George and Peto** to design a palatial new home. He moved into 39 Harrington Gardens in 1883 *(ill. 62)*. This Flemish Gothic fantasy was lavishly decorated inside and equipped with all the latest gadgets including electric light, central heating and a telephone with a direct line to the Savoy Theatre. The doors to the various rooms bore mottoes, such as 'abandon all hope ye who enter here' in the dining room. It was here that Gilbert was to write *Princess Ida, The Mikado, Ruddigore, The Yeomen of the Guard* and *The Gondoliers.*

He moved out in 1890 when he acquired Grimsdyke, a massive pseudo-Tudor manor house at Harrow, where additions and alterations were made for him by **George** and **Peto**. Evidently feeling the need to retain a London base, Gilbert acquired 36 Prince's Gardens but left in 1898 following the failure of the last and only unsuccessful Savoy opera, *The Grand Duke.*

The Goat

The oldest surviving pub on Kensington High Street is the Goat at 3a, opposite the gates into Palace Avenue. The original premises was built in 1695 by a 'coffeeman' but by 1702 had gained its present name and function. The pub was soon joined by a string of small shops, parts of which still remain squeezed in between their newer

66. *The Goat, 3 Kensington High Street, c.1895.*

neighbours. No 19 is a remarkably complete example of the buildings put up in the 1690s.

Early in the 18th century Catherine Dicken and Mary Carnaby left £90 to the parish school. The funds were used to buy the Goat and when this was let out five-eighths of the rent went towards the school's upkeep. Shortly after all benefactions, including rent from the Goat, were merged to help fund **Kensington Charity School**

Rumours abound of secret tunnels linking the pub to Kensington Palace and indeed there are extensive vaults under the road but so far no tunnel has been located.

The pub was extensively altered in 1880 but since then very few structural changes have been made. Attempts to turn the premises into a gastro pub or wine bar have been resisted, a wise decision as it is always very busy and popular with tourists.

67. *George Godwin the Younger.*

George Godwin, The Younger

Godwin (1815-1888) was the prime architect of the **Gunter Estate.** He was born in Brompton and studied architecture under his father, George Godwin the Elder. At twenty the younger Godwin won the first ever medal awarded by the Royal Institute of British Architects for an essay on concrete which was long regarded as a standard authority on the topic, and by the early 1840s he had attained a position of respect and influence in the profession. An expert on the history of Gothic ecclesiastical architecture, he restored a number of medieval buildings and, in 1838, published *The Churches of London*. In 1844 Godwin was appointed editor of *The Builder* and it became the pre-eminent journal for the construction trade. He campaigned for sanitary reform, better housing for the poor and higher ethical standards.

A man of wide cultural interests, Godwin took an active role in the Royal Literary Fund, and became a Fellow of both the Royal Society and the Society of Antiquaries. His hobby was collecting chairs famous people had sat in. Apparently his collection included seats reputedly occupied by Anne Boleyn,

Shakespeare, Napoleon, Sir Walter Raleigh, Alexander Pope, Trollope and **Thackeray**.

His work for Robert Gunter I included the design of **The Boltons** and Godwin continued to work for Robert Gunter's sons, Robert and James, after his death. Godwin was joined by his younger brother, Henry, who became principal architect for the estate in 1888. When George died in 1888 he was buried in **Brompton Cemetery**.

Baron Albert Grant

At the height of his prosperity the amazing Baron Grant (1831-1899) built a princely mansion in Kensington. It was never occupied, except for one night, when the 'Bachelors of London' hired the house from the Baron's creditors and gave a ball of exceptional splendour.

The Baron's real name was Abraham Gottheimer, his father being German and his mother English. By the age of twenty-

69. *Albert Grant, depicted by Ape in Vanity Fair, 1874.*

five he was running his own business and ten years later was MP for Kidderminster. Financial problems prompted him to flee to Italy where he was given

the title of Baron by King Victor Emanuel. On his return in 1870 he embarked on a series of money-making schemes of dubious legality.

It was at this time Grant purchased Colby House and Kensington House to build his palace. To these he added Jennings' Buildings and other rookeries, paying off those who did not leave voluntarily and, by allowing them to take away what they wished of the buildings, saved the cost of clearance. The mansion was said to have cost £250,000 and was unbelievably lavish both inside and out.

However, the Baron was unable to pay the contractor, and the mansion, known as 'Grant's Folly', was pulled down because no one could afford to buy or rent it. The house was reduced to rubble and its salvageable materials were sold off. Few, if any, of the thousands who mount and descend the marble staircase which adorns the entrance-hall of Madame

68. *The new Kensington House, Grant's ostentatious pile in which he never lived.*

49

Tussaud's are aware that it originally formed part of Grant's white elephant. The beautiful iron railings and gates were purchased for the Sandown Park Club, where they may still be seen.

Grant's career is uncannily shadowed in Trollope's *The Way We Live Now* written in 1873 and brilliantly adapted for television in 2001.

Great Exhibition of 1851

The Great Exhibition of the Works of Industry of All Nations, held in Hyde Park, was opened by Queen Victoria on 1 May 1851. The brainchild of her husband and consort Prince Albert, it was a team of engineers, administrators and entrepreneurs

71. *Joseph Paxton.*

spearheaded by **Sir Henry Cole** that made it a reality. It was an outstanding success, attracting some 6 million visitors and making a profit of £186,000 by the

time it closed on 15 October 1851.

The event was to showcase British technological achievements and its place as the leading industrial nation of the world. The objects on display came from all parts of the world, including India, Australia and New Zealand. All were housed in Joseph Paxton's magnificent Crystal Palace, an iron goliath containing over a million feet of glass.

In October the Crystal Palace was taken down and transferred to Sydenham. With the profits the 1851 Commissioners purchased 87 acres of land in the vicinity to create 'a cultural and educational quarter where arts and sciences could be promoted and taught to be of practical use to industry'. It was to radically alter the area, transforming the

70. *The interior of the Great Exhibition in the Crystal Palace in 1851.*

72. The Great Wheel at Earl's Court, c.1904.

73. James Gunter II.

landscape of farms, nurseries, market gardens and orchards into a prosperous metropolitan district of bricks and mortar.

Great Wheel

The Great Wheel, a predecessor of the London Eye, appeared on the Earl's Court skyline in 1894 but survived for little more than a decade. The brain child of **Imre Kiralfy**, it was modelled on the great Ferris wheel in Chicago.

Three hundred feet in diameter and weighing 1,000 tons it took 20 minutes to complete a revolution, plus a short pause to allow passengers to enjoy the view. Each of the forty cars carried 40 people and refreshments were served. *The Builder* thought that the cost should have been "devoted to some more useful end than carrying coach loads of fools round a vertical circle", but the public loved it. A testament to British Victorian engineering, it broke down only once. Passengers were compensated with a £5 note.

The Wheel survived until 1907, when it ceased to be profitable and was broken up, having carried some 2,500,000 passengers during its lifetime.

Gunter Estate

The Gunter Estate of some 100 acres was acquired piecemeal by members of the Gunter family between 1797 and 1866. The north portion ran from Old Brompton Road to Cromwell Road between Gloucester Road and Earl's Court Road; the southern part from Old Brompton Road to Fulham Road between The Boltons and Brompton Cemetery. The Gunters' wealth was founded on their confectionery business in Berkeley Square which was described as "the most celebrated confectioners in London" supplying all the grandest tables in the land. The shop continued in business until 1976.

Initially, James Gunter purchased the land for market gardening purposes which he ran very successfully. Robert, his son, inherited the life interest of the estate and continued to accumulate land including Earl's Court House, the family home for the next sixty years. His main interest was running an innovative market garden business and is believed to have pioneered the first steam heated greenhouses. With the assistance of **George Godwin** he initiated the development of **The Boltons** in 1850, rightly considered the jewel of the estate.

Robert Gunter II inherited the entire estate of his grandfather's while his brother James inherited the portion accumulated by his father. Potentially the situation could have caused friction but they were able to re-apportion the estate between them. Both brothers continued to purchase land but as neither was interested in market gardening, they began to seek other means of capitalising on their lands. They employed the same surveyors, George and Henry **Godwin**, and builders, most notably John Spicer in the northern part and **Corbett and McClymont** in the south. In total, between 1865 and 1895 on sixty acres they erected some 400 houses, twelve mansion blocks and several churches and on the 'Redcliffe Estate' 1100 houses, two churches and five pubs.

After the Crimean war Robert moved to Wetherby Hall in Yorkshire, became an MP and was created a baronet in 1901. James became a career soldier retiring as a Major General in 1887 and also settled in Yorkshire.

In 1917, Robert's son Nevill put his portion up for auction but it failed to reach its reserve. The family continued to hold and develop the estate until 2002 when it was finally sold to an investment group.

Rider Haggard

When the future Sir Henry Rider Haggard (1856-1925) moved into 24 Redcliffe Square in 1888, he had recently completed the trio of novels for which he is best remembered; *King Solomon's Mines* (1885), *She* (1887) and *Allan Quartermain* (1887). Many more were to follow but none approached the success of these

74. H. Rider Haggard, by Spy, 1887.

early ripping yarns, which won him the friendship of Rudyard Kipling and the admiration of Jung. Haggard moved from Redcliffe Square in 1891, and in his later years researched and wrote extensively on agricultural and imperial issues such as forestry and emigration policy.

Anna Marie Hall and Samuel Carter Hall

The Halls moved into The Rosary, one of a pair of villas erected on the north side of Old Brompton Road near the junction with Gloucester Road, in 1839. Samuel Hall (1800-1889), author of *The Baronial Halls and Picturesque Edifices of England*, built a wing on the east side with Gothic windows and decorated in the appropriate baronial style to house their extensive library. An active member of the Temperance Movement he edited the

75. The library in The Rosary.

radical *New Monthly Magazine*. Samuel was also editor of the *Art Journal*. Letters show that he commissioned the photographic pioneer William Henry Fox Talbot, whose work he greatly admired, to provide illustrations. Samuel is thought to be the model for the odious Mr Picksniff in Charles Dickens's *Martin Chuzzlewit*.

His wife, Anna Marie Fielding (1800-1881), was a prolific writer on all manner of subjects including travel guides, plays, children's stories and sketches of Irish life. These sketches, while popular in England, caused controversy in her native Ireland as she managed to offend both Orangemen and Catholics. A devout Christian, she championed causes such as the plight of street musicians and took an active part in the founding of Brompton Hospital, the Governesses' Institution and the delightfully named Home for Decaying Gentlewomen.

They left the Rosary in 1849 and a short time later took up residence at 21 The Boltons.

76. George II, studio of Charles
Jeras, c.1727.

77. Queen Caroline.

House of Hanover in Kensington

In July 1714 Queen Anne fell mortally ill and the vexed question of her successor had to be addressed. Her last act as Queen was to procure the lawful Protestant succession of the House of Hanover. Thus George I became the chatelaine of **Kensington Palace**. Very little good has been said about George but he had grand plans for the old Palace which was in urgent need of repair. The core of the old Jacobean house was replaced, two new courts added and Kent was commissioned to redesign the interiors

Included in the King's entourage was Jory the Dwarf whose behaviour was even worse than his masters – he was imprisoned for molesting a maid and attacking two footmen. Peter the Wildboy, discovered in woods near Hamelin, was brought to England and exhibited as a curiosity. He was often seen roaming the gardens walking on his hands and feet and climbing trees with the agility of a squirrel.

The arrival of George II and Queen Caroline was to usher in the greatest age for Kensington Palace and due to the faithful chronicling of both Lord Hervey and Horace Walpole much of their domestic life here has been recorded. Hervey has written extensively about the family rows, the gossip and tittle-tattle that Caroline adored, especially if it concerned her hated son Frederick, and Court intrigue.

During George's frequent absences he appointed Caroline as sole Regent much to the chagrin of his son. Eventually Frederick was expelled from court and never saw his mother again. George detested his Prime Minister, Robert Walpole, but Caroline persuaded the King to retain him. After Caroline's death, Walpole became equally adept at managing the monarch through his many mistresses.

Queen Caroline had exquisite taste and gave great encouragement to the leading architects and artists of the day. She did much to build up the Royal picture collection. Her other great passion was gardening and in Rocque's maps of Kensington Gardens the results of her work can be seen, including the Broad Walk and the Round Pond.

It was in the gardens in the late 1740s that a chance encounter with another famous Kensington resident took place. The Lady Sarah Lennox, sister of Lady Caroline Holland, broke away from her governess and toddled up to the King on the Broad Walk and, addressing him in perfect French, conquered his heart. She was frequently invited to amuse the old King. Sarah also caught the eye of his grandson, later George III, who continued to court her until his marriage to Princess Charlotte.

Although George II adored his wife he was constantly unfaithful, but consulted her on everything including problems with his mistresses. After Caroline's death in 1737, the King was grief-stricken, closing up large parts of the Palace although he continued to stay there. George died in a small closet in Kensington Palace suddenly on 25 October 1760.

George III told Horace Walpole that he "desired to be excused living at Kensington" and thus the State rooms were closed and for the next 60 years the Palace stood largely empty.

78. Joseph Hansom.

Joseph Aloysius Hansom

Talented and imaginative, Hansom's career was hampered by his inability to complete projects or manage money. Starting out with architect John Oakes in 1825 he learnt Gothic design techniques and met his future partner Edward Welch. They established their own practice in York in 1828, building many churches across England. In 1831 Hansom won a competition to design Birmingham Town Hall. Here he displayed his inventiveness, developing several new building techniques, but chronic bad business sense bankrupted the firm in 1834. That year he patented a design for his famous cab, but it was a John Chapman who in 1836 modified Hansom's design to the form which became standard throughout the country. Hansom had the driver sitting at the front of the roof, whereas Chapman shifted him to the rear, which became the common version. But by then the impecunious Hansom had sold his rights to the cab which bore his name to another company for £10,000, but they defaulted on payment and Hansom received nothing for his invention.

He also founded *The Builder*, a journal full of pioneering ideas, but was sacked as editor after a year for nearly bankrupting it. Finally he set up partnership with his second son in 1869 before retiring in 1879.

Hansom (1803-1882) lived in Kensington from 1863 until his death. Starting in Neville Terrace in 1863 he also lived in Thurloe Street twice, Sumner Place and Fulham Road. He died at his Fulham Road home in 1882 and is buried in St Thomas' Church in Fulham.

Harrington Estate

The 87 acres of the Harrington Villars estate roughly covers the Queen's Gate area and sits between the **Gunter** and **Alexander** estates. The land passed through several hands including Sir William Blake who acquired Hale House, which stood where Queen's Gate crosses the Cromwell Road, and the surrounding land in 1606. The next owner was William Methwold, followed by Sir John Fleming who added the northern parts of the Queen's Gate area.

On Fleming's death the estate was shared by his two daughters: Seymour Dorothy who married a Swiss and moved to Paris owned the Villars portion, and Jane who married Charles Stanhope, 3rd Lord Harrington, the remainder. In 1850 the Court of Chancery formally approved a division of the land and the Villars family sold their portion to the 1851 Commissioners.

Some of the finest architects and builders were employed such as C J Richardson, William Jackson and Charles Aldin. They were responsible for the magnificent houses on the west side of Queen's Gate, Queen's Gate Terrace and Place, parts of Gloucester Road, Elvaston and Petersham Place.

In 1957 most of the Harrington lands, with the exception of 12 acres, were sold by 11th Earl of Harrington.

Rolf Harris

In 1952 a young Australian, Rolf Harris (b. 1930), stepped off the ferry at Dover with dreams of being a famous portrait painter. He could also play the piano, write songs, ride a bike with no hands and swim 110 yards backstroke in eighty seconds. In his autobiography, *Can you tell what it is yet?*, he writes about meeting some South African dentists on board the ferry to England, a meeting which was to prove very useful to him later. When he first arrived, he stayed in a YMCA, but having to find somewhere else to live he remembered his South African friends and turned up on their doorstep in Earl's Court unannounced. He spent the next few days sleeping on the floor in his raincoat. This inauspicious beginning in **Kangaroo Valley** was the start of a multifarious career for him, making it understandable why he is called a Renaissance Man. Whilst still living in Earl's Court he made his debut at the Down Under Club in Fulham. Later he went on to further fame as a children's TV presenter, pop star and headline act at Glastonbury as well as painting a portrait of the Queen, involvement in animal hospitals and much more.

79. The first Harrods store in Brompton Road before replacement by the present building.

80. Richard Burbidge, managing director of Harrods.

Harrods

Harrods, often dubbed the world's greatest store, is the only department store that began life as a grocery shop. Its reputation and motto is providing "Everything for Everybody Everywhere". In 1849 Charles Harrod bought a grocery shop in Brompton Road. His son took over in 1861 and expanded it, selling a wider range of goods including perfumes, furniture and china. From these beginnings, the store has grown vastly in both size and diversity. Today, it is one of the most visited tourist attractions in London.

In 1889 the thriving store became a public limited company. It had a staff of 200. Expansion was rapid in the next two decades under managing director Richard Burbidge. By 1902, when the first section of its famous terracotta frontage was completed, there were 91 departments and more than 2000 staff. Harrods introduced Britain's first escalator and pioneered telephone shopping. By 1911 Harrods occupied the whole island site.

Through the 1920s and 1930s Harrods remained London's biggest and most elegant store. The rear and centre of the building were redeveloped with sleek interiors for menswear and fashion departments. In 1959 Harrods was acquired by House of Fraser. Following a take-over by the Fayed brothers it reverted to the status of a private company in 1986.

Hereford Lodge and Hereford House

These two houses are frequently confused or considered one and the same, especially as they both lay along the Old Brompton Road.

The first to be built, in the 1760s, was Hereford Lodge on the Day Estate and stood on the site now covered by Brechin Place. The grounds were extensive and are now covered by Hereford Square. Prior to that four villas were put up in the grounds. Famous residents of the Lodge included the diva, Gertrude Elisabeth Mara, the daughters of the 2nd Duke of

Roxburghe and the Rev. George Stokes, rector of Thurloe Chapel. In 1869 Walter Woodbury, inventor of a photographic reproducing process, set up a studio in the grounds which survived until 1876. All were pulled down in the 1880s but are remembered in the street names.

81. Dion Boucicault, one-time resident of Hereford House.

82. Georgette Heyer.

Georgette Heyer

A writer of historical romances, her feisty heroines and dashing heroes overcome adversities to find true love in the colourful Regency period, of whose manners, idiom and lifestyle, Heyer (1902-1974) acquired an undisputedly expert knowledge. Her best known works are *Devil's Cub* (1934) and *Regency Buck* (1935). The latter includes a description of **Tattersall's** where the heroine, Judith Taverner is taken by her aristocratic guardian to buy a matched pair of carriage-horses. Heyer also developed an interest in detective novels. In *Duplicate Death* her ex-convict heroine lives in a flat off Cromwell Road, where Heyer and her barrister husband had their first marital home.

Alfred Hitchcock

Hitchcock (1899-1989) had an authoritarian father, who had him locked in a police cell at the age of five. He was shy and reclusive with a strict Catholic upbringing, and commentators

Hereford House was erected in the garden of Coleherne House in 1815 on the **Gunter Estate**. It was described by **Beatrix Potter**, who lived next door as 'the red house'. Members of the theatrical profession obviously approved as the burlesque writer Charles Dance, the theatrical manager Benjamin Lumley and the actor dramatist Dion Boucicault all lived there. His daughter, Nina Boucicault, was the first actress to take the part of Peter Pan staged at the Duke of York's in 1904.

Just before the house was demolished to make way for **Coleherne Court** it was used as a Ladies' Cycling Club. Races were held on Saturdays and the track was described as 'a miniature Olympian'. One commentator approved "Scores of ladies are to be seen riding about with such ease and grace as to convince even the most prejudiced that ladies could look elegant on bicycles".

83. Alfred Hitchcock.

draw links between his childhood and his work. Other influences include a love of Edgar Allan Poe, films and his wife. He married film editor Alma Reville in 1926, a major partner and collaborator in his career. They had one daughter.

Starting in Germany in 1924 as an assistant on *The Blackguard*, he later directed *The Pleasure Garden* and *The Mountain Eagle*. Signing for Gainsborough Studios in England he produced critically acclaimed films like *The Lodger* inspired by German theatrical and effect-driven techniques. He moved to British International Pictures in 1927 then Gaumont-British in 1934, producing films jsuch as *Blackmail*, *The 39 Steps* and *The Lady Vanishes*. His best work came after moving to America in 1937. Starting with *Rebecca* he went on to direct hit after hit, including the seminal *Psycho*. Hitchcock was honoured with the American Institute's Life Time Achievement Award in 1979.

Cromwell Road was the family home throughout Hitchcock's English career. Designed by him and decorated by studio technicians it became a second studio. He spent as much time here as on set during the making of a film, believing a laid-back approach produced the most realistic scripts. Asked about working with Hitchcock most scriptwriters mention two things, his dining room and his silk pyjamas.

Holy Trinity

As the population of Kensington began to increase in the 1820s, first the Kensington Vestry and subsequently the Church Commissioners saw the need for an additional church to **St Mary Abbots**. There was much argument as to which end of the parish should be favoured, but **Brompton** was chosen. Holy Trinity was given a large parish running as far west as Earl's Court and Stamford Bridge. Later an increase in funds, voted by Parliament, made it possible to erect St Barnabas, Addison Road to serve the west of the parish.

The cost of buying the Holy Trinity site, previously a burial ground for St George's Hospital, and building the church came to nearly £10,734. The Commissioners for Building New Churches contributed £7,407 and Kensington parish provided the balance. The architect was Thomas Leverton Donaldson and building, in the plain Gothic style, started in 1826. The setting of the church, approached by an avenue of trees, is surprisingly secluded considering its position just off the busy Brompton Road. The church was consecrated on 6 June 1829 and provided seats for 1,505 people, of which 899 were rented and 606 free.

Today, Holy Trinity, better known as HTB, is the centre for the new evangelical movement and the Alpha Course. This is a programme designed to introduce people to the basics of Christianity and were laid down by the Rev. Charles Marnham when he was a curate at Holy Trinity in 1979. Appealing primarily to the 18-35 age group, the message is spread through groups meeting in private houses for food and religious discussion and then to other churches. Detractors describe these as 'happy-clappy' churches and some liberals are increasingly concerned about the simplistic approach of the teachings. However it is highly successful and is countering the trends of declining and ageing congregations and cash crises.

Hotels and Tourism

In 1851 visitors flocked to Kensington in their thousands and have continued to do so ever since. In 2005 around 17 million people visited the Borough, many of them on day trips, and spent £2 billion. The main draws are the museums of South Kensington, which all feature in the top ten attractions in London, **Kensington Palace**, Notting Hill Carnival and **Harrods**.

An abundance of accommodation, some 90,000 beds, central location and good transport links makes the area a suitable place to stay. Of the 191 hotels, ranging from some of the best in London such as The Royal Garden Hotel to the very basic, 97 are to be found in Earl's Court and Queen's Gate. Latest figures indicate that £1.5 million was spent on hotel accommodation. Related business such as shops, bars, restaurants also benefit greatly from this influx, creating excellent employment opportunities. Unsurprisingly, the Council sees tourism as one of the primary business activities within the Borough.

John Hunter

John Hunter (1728-1793), one of the most eminent surgeons of his day, took a ninety-year lease on three pieces of land in Earl's Court in 1765. He used Earl's Court House as a retreat from the fatigues of his profession but in no respect from his labours

84. John Hunter.

which were "to pursue his studies in comparative anatomy by making experiments upon animals and vegetables."

A large menagerie was assembled including buffalo (often to be seen pulling carts between Earl's Court and Town), rams, sheep from Turkey, shawl goats from East Indies, a jackal, zebra, ostrich, two leopards, eagles attached to rocks and snakes. Edward Jenner and sailors disembarking at Chelsea Reach provided these specimens. Hunter also obtained the privilege of first refusal on exotic beasts which had expired at the Tower of London menagerie, and he accumulated a collection of 13,600 stuffed specimens and skeletons. He built cloisters leading to his laboratory so that the long-suffering Mrs Hunter would not be disturbed by these activities.

One such specimen was the corpse of the Irish giant, Byrne O'Brien, for which Hunter paid £500 to the 'resurrection men'. The skeleton was prepared in large copper kettles and today still hangs in the Royal College of Surgeons.

Earl's Court House was de-

85. A music cover, designed by Thomas Packer, for the Great International Exhibition quadrille, 1862.

molished in 1886 to make way for the building of Barkston Gardens.

International Exhibition 1862

The International Exhibition of 1862 continued the tradition of showing how art and manufacture can be intertwined. The building was designed by **Captain Francis Fowke** and built by Sir John Kerk on the 23-acre site

86. The building erected for the Great International Exhibition, 1862.

now occupied by the **Natural History Museum**. The exhibition, intended to both stimulate trade and have popular appeal, also included the Fine Arts.

Prince Albert was unable to commit himself as much as he would have liked due to health problems, and despite his death on 14 December 1861 the Exhibition building was handed over to the organisers on 12 February 1862, within the assigned deadline.

Thirty-nine countries participated and separate sections featured machinery in motion, carriages and cabs, groups of statuary, displays of jewellery including the Kohinoor diamond, gold and silver plate and an impressive array of armaments.

Financially the Exhibition was not a success, receipts falling £10,000 short of expenditure. The building was derided in the *Building News* as "one of the ugliest buildings ever raised in the country". It was taken down and sold for scrap. Further exhibitions were held annually between 1871 and 1874 and 1883 to 86, but none could match the success of the **Great Exhibition**.

Ismaili Centre

The Ismaili Centre (pictured on the back cover of this book) was opened in 1979 in Thurloe Place with the aim of serving the requirements of the Aga Khan's Ismaili community while establishing a presence worthy of its illustrious neighbours. Margaret Thatcher in her opening speech acknowledged that many of the Centre members were East Africans, expelled by Idi Amin from Uganda. She added, "they have made Britain their new home, triumphed over these adversities and have found here a new sense of security and belonging".

The island of land between Thurloe Place and Cromwell Road, opposite the Victoria & Albert Museum was originally intended to be the site for the National Theatre. George Bernard Shaw laid the foundation stone here in 1939 but the plans came to nothing. The plot lay derelict for years until the Aga Khan spotted its potential especially as it conveniently faces south-east towards Mecca.

The architect Neville Conder was given the challenge to design a building that represented Islamic art and culture, as well as reflecting British cultural tradition. He lived in nearby Thurloe Square as well as having offices in Thurloe Place, and so he came with a unique knowledge of the site and its environment.

Built in white polished granite with hundreds of teak framed panes of panelled glass the exterior is both elegant and striking. The centre piece of the interior, designed by Karl Schlamminger, a German Muslim, is a vast Prayer Hall. This is capable of accommodating 1,250 worshippers and is accessed via an entrance hall with a seven-sided fountain, seven-sided pillars and a geometric stone floor.

The Roof Garden, on the third floor, is one of London's best kept secrets. The beautiful and peaceful garden, with its emphasis on natural elements of water, plants and birds, is intended to give 'spiritual balm' for the soul.

Kangaroo Valley

Many would be forgiven for thinking in the 1960s that **Earl's Court** was a suburb of Sydney or Melbourne; Bed-sit Jungle had turned into Kangeroo Valley.

After the War once respectable houses were turned into bed-sits and cheap hotels and a distinctly Bohemian atmosphere pervaded the area. In 1955 the Overseas Visitors Club welcomed more than 100,000 visitors at British ports and brought them to Earl's Court where they organised tours, accommodation and work. The Australian contingent was made up of two groups; the professionals who came to study and 'make it' in this country and the young backpackers. Notable names

87. *Fanny Kemble.*

Sarah Siddons, Fanny was not intended for the boards, but educated at a genteel academy at 22 Hans Place. Fellow pupils included writer Laetitia Landon and Caroline Lamb, future lover of Lord Byron. At twenty, however, Fanny found herself obliged to act to save her father from bankruptcy. Her Juliet was a sensation, launching a brief but highly successful career. She left the stage in 1834 to marry a wealthy American admirer and moved to the USA. Discovering that she loathed slavery, the basis of her husband's fortune, Fanny divorced him and re-launched herself on a new career, giving readings from Shakespeare. Settling in London in 1868 she produced eight volumes of autobiography. She left Hereford Square in 1890.

Kensington Charity School

Two painted stone figures of a boy and a girl on the north front of St Mary Abbots School, Kensington Church Court are all that remain of the Charity School

88. *Hawksmoor's Kensington Charity School.*

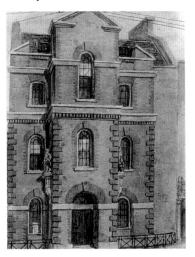

arriving in this first wave include Barry Humphries *aka* Dame Edna, Germaine Greer, Peter Finch, Clive James, John Pilger, Joan Sutherland and **Rolf Harris**.

By the 1960s there was an eclectic mix of clean-cut 'colonials', hippies and beatniks plus, of course, bemused often elderly locals. Late night clubs, pubs and cheap eateries proliferated all vying to serve this new and lucrative market. *Time Out* referred to Earl's Court as "a neighbourhood of strangers washed over by a steamy monsoon of laundro-mats." With the increase in air travel and the convenience of the Piccadilly line, new arrivals headed straight for Earl's Court. Agencies such as Trailfinders grew up to cater for the newcomers, mainly working holidaymakers planning to party and travel.

Local concerns, especially about overcrowding and drink and drug abuse, grew leading to action to reduce the bed numbers. Prices rose and the Australians moved on to other areas.

Fanny Kemble

By the time Fanny Kemble (1809-1893) moved into 26 Hereford Square in 1884, she was a theatrical legend, long since retired. Born into a formidable theatrical dynasty, daughter of Charles Kemble and niece of the famous

89. An entrance to Kensington Place and Gardens; watercolour attributed to Princess Sophia.

90. Sheep shearing in Kensington Gardens, c.1893.

designed by Nicholas Hawksmoor.

Queen Anne was among the subscribers of the first school whose pupils wore distinctive blue uniforms topped off with blue caps with crimson tassels and strings. On leaving children were apprenticed or put into domestic service and sent out with a Bible and a copy of *The Whole Duty of Man*.

In 1709 the school was re-built. Hawksmoor's design had a three story red-brick frontage with a central bell tower and separate entrances for boys and girls marked by the relevant painted statue. Soon extra accommodation was required and a new girls' school was built next door. When the Church took over the administration it became a National School and further extensions were made at the rear into Church Court.

It was to this site that the whole school was moved in 1875 when the Hawksmoor building was demolished to make way for a **Vestry Hall**, later Kensington's first Town Hall.

Kensington Gardens

Despite its name and contrary to most people's opinion Kensington Gardens lies for the most part in the City of Westminster, only the small part west of the Broad Walk falls within the Royal Borough's boundaries.

The grounds were originally attached to Nottingham House and came into Royal hands when William and Mary pur-chased the house as their winter palace. They took a great interest in the gardens and commissioned London and Wise to lay them out in the Dutch style. The next resident, Queen Anne, left two great legacies – the splendid Orangery, designed by Hawksmoor and modified by Vanbrugh, and the landscaped gardens of today's Kensington Gardens, the work of Wise and Charles Bridgeman. The Broad Walk, the avenues of elms, the Queen's Temple, the Serpentine and the Round Pond, built for keeping tortoises, are the work of Queen Caroline.

In 1733 the Gardens were opened to "respectably dressed people" on Saturdays but only when the Royals were not in residence. The Broad Walk became a very fashionable place to promenade. It was William IV who opened the park to the public all the year round. Improvements then continued apace with new flower beds, statues and play areas added. In the 1950s many of the elms became diseased and had to be replaced; further damage was sustained in the Great Storm of 1987.

Today the Gardens are particularly popular for sunbathing

91. *Pupils and teacher at Kensington Grammar School, 1880.*

and picnicking in fine weather and by dog owners all year round. Children still enjoy the Round Pond, Peter Pan's statue and Elfin Oak but now also flock to the Diana, Princess of Wales' Memorial Playground for a visit to Never, Never Land. Commuters use it as a healthy walking route to work and cyclists have designated paths. But above all Kensington Gardens is a peaceful refuge for people living, working or visiting the area.

Kensington Grammar School

Hidden in the depths of Kensington Central Library, sits the wall plaque which once graced the front of Kensington Grammar School at 27 Kensington Square. In 1831 the Kensington Proprietary Grammar School was established at no 31, but it soon expanded into no 27 where there was space for a cricket pitch and playground in the

garden. Teaching was by a monitoring system, older boys, instructed by teachers, passing on their knowledge to younger pupils. By 1841 this was abandoned and boys were prepared for the East India Company's schools at Haileybury and Addiscombe. New subjects such as Hindustani, military drawing, fortification and drill were

introduced. The school flourished and expanded acquiring nos. 25, 26, 28 and 29 along the way. The arrival of the railway, which cut off a large portion of the grounds, led to a decline and the school was taken over by one of the Assistant Masters, the Rev. Charles Ackland. He opened the Kensington Foundation School in 1873 which flour-

92. *Kensington High Street, c.1905, looking west from the old Vestry Hall. The entrance to the tube is on the left by the lamp post.*

93. *Kensington High Street, c.1905, looking east. In the centre stands the Queen Victoria Memorial, funded by local residents. In 1934 it was moved to Warwick Gardens.*

ished until it succumbed in 1896 to competition from St Paul's School in Hammersmith.

The houses were taken over by the Crown and leased to Derry & Toms for warehousing and staff accommodation. Today they are once more private houses.

Kensington High Street

During the 19th century Kensington High Street changed from a village street to a bustling commercial centre. Department stores, hotels, railway lines, shops, people, houses and carriages all competed for space on this famous road. In 1854 the *Kensington Gazette* reported that "the High Street was rapidly improving. Several old buildings have been replaced by new and handsome houses, while the mean and narrow fronts of many shops are giving way to glass and brass ..." In 1870 the *Kensington News* enthused that there were now, "55 superb newly built shops on the south side of the High Street." By the end of 19th century it was the department stores and banks that dominated the High Street with many smaller traders unable to compete.

It is still a vibrant place to shop, eat and drink. Sadly Barker's, Derry & Toms and Kensington Market have closed, but the gaps have been or are being filled and eager shoppers have returned.

The Council is undertaking a major refurbishment and upgrade of the High Street with new York stone pavements and modern lampposts making it an even more attractive place to visit.

Kensington Market

Once a 'sixties hangout, and then a venue for small boutiques, Kensington Market was closed in 2001 and then demolished. It was based at 49-53 Kensington High Street, once Story & Co.'s furnishing store which was damaged in a serious fire in 1947.

Famous for unusual clothing, it was a mecca for those looking for gothic, punk or alternative fashion. **Freddie Mercury** and Roger Taylor from Queen are rumoured to have run a clothes stall there.

When the Market closed, petitions were signed but to no avail – the new owners of the site had other plans. For three years the site was left derelict and boarded up with a few traders clinging on the perimeter. The new building now houses a glitzy computer retailer.

Kensington New Town

"It is all very clean and neat and astonishes visitors who a few years ago beheld scarcely a house on the spot." This is how Leigh Hunt, author of *The Old Court Suburb*, described Kensington New Town. This charming enclave of moderate individual villas was built between 1839 and 1845 on land east of Victoria Grove. Unusually, instead of a uniform development in white stucco, the houses in streets such as Canning Place, Victoria Grove and Launceston Place are varied in size and shape.

Built on former nursery ground, it was conceived as a suburb of Kensington and planned as a 'township'. This included a church, shops and semi-detached villas similar to Camden New Town which was developed at the same time. Two merchants Howell Leny Valloton and John Inderwick were responsible for the development. The Valloton family, which acquired the estate in the late 18th century, made their fortune from haberdashery and fancy goods and lived in Rutland Lodge, Addison Road.

94. *Kensington Palace, a print published during the reign of William and Mary.*

The Inderwick family were tobacconists and snuff merchants who had been in business in Wardour Street since 1811. The firm, Inderwick and Company, tobacconists, survived in Carnaby Street until 1998.

Famous residents include sculptor Alfred Stephens, at 7 Canning Place; the painter Samuel Palmer, at 6 Douro Place; poet Sir Henry Newbolt, at 14 Victoria Road; Sir George Robey, the 'Prime Minister of Mirth', at 10 Victoria Road and animal painter Alfred Corbould at 52 Victoria Road and in the 1960s the couturier, Sir Hardy Amies at 17 Eldon Road.

Kensington Palace

What stories the walls of Kensington Palace could tell. Since 1689 when William and Mary took Nottingham House as their winter Palace Royalty have lived here. This once modest Jacobean villa built by Sir George Coppin in *c.* 1610 has been altered and enlarged by some of the country's foremost architects, beginning with Sir Christopher Wren.

It ceased to be the monarch's official residence on the accession of George III who moved to Buckingham Palace. After further alterations by James Wyatt it was used by George's sons the **Dukes of Kent and Sussex**.

They were soon joined by the estranged wife of the Prince of Wales, Caroline of Brunswick.

Queen Mary, wife of George V, was born here in 1867. According to Lord Esher they planned to pull down Buckingham Palace and sell part of St. James's Palace, and with the money reconstruct Kensington as the town residence of the Sovereign. This, was to remain just a dream. Instead Kensington became a Royal rest home referred to as the 'Aunt Heap' with Princesses Beatrice and Alice, Victoria's daughters, joining Princess Louise who had been in residence since 1880.

Margaret, in the '70s by Prince and Princess Michael of Kent and of course most famously in the '80s by the Prince and Princess of Wales.

Kensington Palace Gardens

Once the kitchen garden of **Kensington Palace** today Kensington Palace Gardens, or as it is more often known, Millionaires' Row, is one of the world's most expensive streets. In 1838, Queen Victoria decided to sell the land to finance improvements in Windsor Castle. By 1870, it was as *The Illustrated London News* predicted 'the most aristocratic neighbourhood.'

The Earl Harrington lived at no 13. In the 1871 census, his widow was listed as having twenty servants, a dairy, laundry, still room, wine room, dung house and dust pit. In 1930 the Soviet government acquired the lease, the first of many diplomatic arrivals. By the 1970s the Soviets had a number of other houses on the road.

Next door at no 12, Sir Samuel Morton Peto MP, railway entrepreneur, built a house large enough to accommodate 28 people, but this was not large enough so he built an even grander dwelling next door. George Moore said he only built no. 15 to please his wife and described it as 'both wicked and aggrandising, mere ostentation and vain show.' In 1937, No. 15 was remodelled for the philanthropist, Sir Alfred Beit. The panels in the dining room at one time contained Murillo's painting of the *Parable of the Prodigal Son*. Cyril Mills, the circus owner, lived at no. 17 and allegedly spied on the Russians next door for MI5. Julius de Reuter, founder of the news agency, occupied no. 18 from 1868 till his death in 1899. He too found the original too small adding a billiard room and an art gallery.

Today over half of the 35 houses are owned by individuals, a mixture of industrialists, financiers and minor royalty, but this is a recent trend. There are still eight embassies and several ambassadorial residences. A world

In 1889 the State Apartments were opened to the public to mark Victoria's 70th birthday and the Queen used the occasion to make her final visit to her birthplace. From 1950 to 1975 the apartments were used by the London Museum, in which exhibits included Queen Mary's Dolls' House, now at Windsor.

During the war the Palace was hit twice and considerably damaged, and it was to take several years to repair for use once more as a residence for members of the Royal family. The first to arrive in 1955 was Princess Marina and her children, followed in the '60s by Princess

95. *The Earl of Harrington's mansion in Kensington Palace Gardens. From* The Builder, *June 1852.*

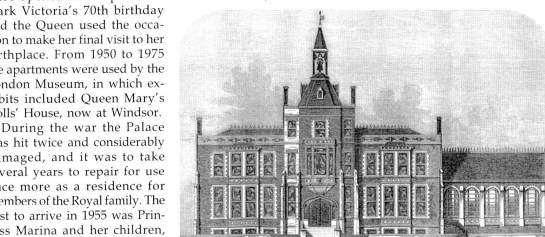

96. *The mansion of Sir Samuel Morton Peto in Kensington Palace Gardens. From* The Builder, *September 1865.*

97. *Kensington Palace Gardens, c.1905.*

Kensington Society

The first Kensington Society was formed in 1865 by eleven women as a discussion group. Nine of them were unmarried and attempting to pursue careers in education or medicine. The group included Barbara Bodichon, Emily Davies, Frances Mary Buss, Dorothea Beale, Anne Clough, Helen Taylor and Elizabeth Garrett.

At one of the meetings the women discussed parliamentary reform. They thought it was unfair that women were not allowed to vote in parliamentary elections and drafted a petition asking Parliament to grant women the vote. The women took their petition to Henry Fawcett and **John Stuart Mill**, two MPs who supported universal suffrage. Mill added an amendment to the Reform Act that would give women the same

record price of £70 million was paid by Lakshmi Mittal for a 99-year lease on nos. 18 and 19, purchased allegedly from Bernie Ecclestone. Other neighbours include members of the Saudi royal family and the Sultan of Brunei. Perhaps it should be renamed Billionaires' Row.

political rights as men; it was defeated by 196 votes to 73.

Kensington Society members were very disappointed when they heard the news and they decided to form the London Society for Women's Suffrage. Similar societies were formed in other large towns in Britain. Eventually seventeen of these groups joined together to form the National Union of Women's Suffrage Societies, better known as **Suffragettes**.

The present Kensington Society was founded in 1953 by Mrs Gay Christiansen. The key objective of the Society is "to preserve and improve the amenities of Kensington for the public benefit". It was formed to fight off the many, often brutal, plans put forward by the London County Council in the 1950s and early '60s. Successes included saving the artists studios in Melbury Road, Leighton House and Tower House from the wrecking ball – only Watts' studio was lost – and the retention of the remains of Holland House, including the Orangery. Other battles have been lost such as the Campden Hill water tower. They also organise an active programme of events including visits and lectures. An annual school essay competition is held to help encourage an interest in local history.

Kensington Square

The most famous residential address in Kensington must be Kensington Square and it still lives up to Daniel Defoe's description of this 'noble square full of good houses'. Built by **Thomas Young** the first known resident was Nicholas Bagnall in 1687 and following the arrival of the Court to Kensington all the houses were occupied by 1696.

The history of the Square has been recounted many times and as many of the famous names and institutions based here are described separately the less familiar will be included here.

Although disparagingly described by Angela Thirkell as 'a common gin palace' the Greyhound at no. 1 has a long and

98. Kensington Square in the 1920s.

99. *The Greyhound in Kensington Square, c.1870.*

distinguished history. An inn of this name is known to have existed since 1710 when Benjamin Jackman took out an insurance policy on the Greyhound Tavern but it is known to have existed at least ten years before that. The Manor courts were sometimes held here in the eighteenth century. In 1805 the freehold was bought by two brewers Harvey Christian Combe and Joseph Delafield, whose present-day successors, Watney Mann, still own the property. The present building was put up in 1899. It was seriously damaged in 1977 by a gas explosion, but it has since been restored.

Numbers 11 and 12 are the best preserved of all the houses in the Square and together with number 13 were taken by The Ladies' Department of King's College in 1908 when it was renamed King's College for Women. They left in 1915 for accommodation on Campden Hill. Soon after their departure the houses were commandeered by the War Supply Depot. Here female volunteers wearing nurses' caps and aprons rolled bandages, produced splints, slings and other surgical aids and dressings from material donated by the public. A report of the depot states, "Were it not for such work the wounded would have no recovery".

The more recent history of the Square is dominated by the residents' fight to keep the mighty **Barker's** at bay. Although there had been early skirmishes, it was Barkers' plan to buy **Thackeray's** house and those owned by the **Merrimans** to build a loading bay that really galvanised all the residents. The battle was fully engaged when Kensington Planning Committee declared in 1946 that there was no reason for the preservation of the buildings on either architectural or historical grounds. Happily this was rejected by the Council and in 1968 Kensington Square became the Borough's second Conservation Area.

100. *The Kensington Turnpike, c. 1806.*

Kensington Turnpike Trust

Charging a fee for travelling into central London by road is by no means a modern phenomenon. By the mid-eighteenth century, anyone entering the city had to pay their way through the numerous gates and tolls erected by Turnpike Trusts. The term 'turnpike' derives from the spiked barricade used for defence in medieval times.

In the early years of the 18th century hundreds of Turnpike Trusts were established by Acts of Parliament to manage the main roads with money collected at tollgates. The Kensington Turnpike Trust was formed in 1726 to maintain the road from Hyde Park Corner to Addison Bridge. In 1811 Joseph Salway, surveyor to the Trust, produced a beautiful set of drawings of the road complete with elevations of the buildings along the road. The Vestry had responsibility for maintaining footpaths and minor roads.

The Trust erected tollgates at key junctions and supposedly the fees collected were to be used to build, maintain and light the roads. Many complaints were made plus the usual accusations of corruption. In common with other such trusts it became notorious for crooked dealings and was frequently attacked in newspapers and broadsheets. Tollgates were situated at junctions that were impossible to avoid such as that at Palace Gate and Kensington Church Street. Traders complained that toll roads kept customers away and the customers complained that the tolls led to an increase in prices; complaints not unfamiliar today in connection with newer toll schemes. Henry Fox went so far as to reposition the entrance gates to Holland House to avoid paying tolls on his journey to Town. There was general rejoicing when the last tollgate was removed in 1869.

Edward, Duke of Kent

The first Duke of Kent to be allocated apartments at **Kensington Palace** was Edward Augustus (1767-1820), fourth son of George III. In 1817 the Prince of Wales's beloved daughter and only child, Princess Charlotte, died in childbirth. Public pressure was put on the other brothers to produce an heir to the throne to succeed the Prince Regent. Edward was the only one of the brothers to seize the opportunity. Banishing his current mistress to a nunnery, he married Princess Victoria of Saxe-Coburg and in 1819 he brought his heavily pregnant wife from Germany to his apartments at Kensington. On May 24 1819 a daughter, Alexandrina **Victoria** was born.

The Duke of Kent, impecunious as ever, died nine months later and the little Princess, now fifth in line, was brought up by her widowed mother at Kensington. William IV was fond of Victoria but loathed her mother, a rift which was deepened by the intrigues of Sir John Conway, the Duchess's chamberlain and alleged lover. During a secret visit to the Palace, William was incensed to find that the Duchess had annexed an extra seventeen rooms and launched a furious and bitter attack on her.

In 1955, Princess Marina, widow of Prince George of Kent, brought her three children, Edward, Alexandra and Michael to live at the Palace in 1955. In 1968 she died of a brain tumour at Kensington. Prince Edward and Prince Michael of Kent continue to live at the Palace with their families although from time to time questions are raised in Parliament as to whether they should continue to enjoy their 'grace and favour' apartments

Madame Kate Ker-Lane

Dr. Dudfield, Kensington's Medical Officer of Health, was a pioneer in the field of public health. He appointed the first female factory inspectors in London and had a good record in safeguarding workers by ensuring employers complied with safety rules. Madame Ker-Lane, a fashionable dressmaker at 3 Kensington High Street, was to have first hand experience of their efficiency. In 1905 she was summoned by factory inspectors for dangerous overcrowding. Forty-three dressmakers were found to be working on four floors and basement of the narrow building with "hardly any light on the stairs and in some places no hand rails".

Imre Kiralfy

The purchase of the lease of the site of **Earl's Court Exhibition** by Hungarian showman Imre Kiralfy (1845-1919) in 1894 was to usher in a new and even more spectacular era. He had learnt his trade with Barnum and Bailey in the USA and at Olympia. Kiralfe replaced most of the buildings and introduced new attractions, the most impressive being the Queen's Court, the Empress Theatre and the **Great Wheel**.

His first exhibition was the Empire of India exhibition which included an Indian village imported from Poona, 200 native craftsmen, a herd of elephants from Burma and a jun-

101. Poster depicting Imre Kiralfy's Victorian Era

gle of stuffed animals. His reign lasted until 1903 and these years were the heyday for the grounds. Kiralfy went on to devote himself to the new exhibition venue at White City.

Robert Machray in his book *The Night Side of London* (1902) gives fulsome praise to Kiralfy contribution, "The Director General of Earl's Court (a native of Buda-Pest) is a man who has a veritable Oriental love of gorgeous display and sensuous magnificence".

102. *The north side of Knightsbridge in 1820, depicting the buildings from Cannon Brewery to Hyde Park Corner.*

Knightsbridge

Once the haunt of highwaymen and celebrated for its many taverns today Knightsbridge is one of the most exclusive addresses in London. Unlike most other hamlets, Knightsbridge straddled several parishes and is still divided between Westminster, Kensington and Chelsea. The name dates back to the 11th century. The legend is that two knights fought to the death on a bridge over the Westbourne, close to the present Albert Gate, hence the name.

Residents in the 18th century still preferred to say they lived in Brompton as it sounded more respectable. Early in the 19th century the situation changed as elegant squares and fine mansions were built. Today the area is best known for its exclusive stores especially Harvey Nichols and **Harrods**.

William Lecky

William Edward Hartpole Lecky (1872-1903) was born in Dublin but travelled widely during his youth. At Trinity College, Dublin he joined the Historical Society, founded by Edmund Burke, and made many friends, including future politicians David Plunket, Edward Gibson and Gerald Fitzgibbon. He married Catherine van Dedem, lady-in-waiting to Queen Sophia of the Netherlands, in 1871. The wedding reception was held at the Dutch court.

Early failures with poetry and his collection of essays *The Leaders of Public Opinion in Ireland* did not discourage Lecky. In 1865 he published *The History of the Rise and Influence of the Spirit of Rationalism in Europe* that examined Christianity's involvement in European development. A huge hit it was published 15 times in his lifetime. Other philosophical histories followed, including his famous *History of England* (1878-90). Lecky entered politics in 1895 as Ulster Unionist MP for Dublin University, rejecting his previous Home Rule stance. He supported rule from Westminster, Irish landowners and prisoners' rights and the removal of religion from politics.

103. *William Lecky, albumen print by Julia Margaret Cameron, 1868.* © *National Portrait Gallery, London.*

Returning to London from his honeymoon Lecky settled at 38 Onslow Gardens. Guests at his home included Carlyle, **Leslie Stephen**, Robert Browning, Tennyson, Lord Derby, and Herbert Spencer. While here he was elected to the Literary Society in 1873 and The Club, founded by Dr Johnson, in 1874.

John Lennon

At the height of Beatlemania, John Lennon (1940-1980) moved into Flat 3, 13 Emperor's Gate with his wife Cynthia and son Julian in 1963 under the pseudonym Hadley. The flat was recommended by Robert Freeman, photographer for many of the Beatle album covers, who lived in Flat 2. Despite the pseudonym, the address soon became known to fanatical fans who besieged the entrance both day and night. By July 1964 the family, and doubtless other residents, had had enough and the family left London for Weybridge. The row of houses, including no. 13, were demolished in the 1980s to make way for an office block.

Library history

By the late 19th century the Industrial Revolution brought riches to a new rising middle class, whilst Mechanics' Institutes and the Workers' Educational Association were also bringing education and the love of reading to the working classes. Public Libraries were seen by many Victorians to be essential in ensuring access to the world of knowledge. Many of the first public libraries consisted only of newspaper reading rooms and reference books, and it wasn't until the demise of the Boots circulating library that fiction was generally available in public libraries.

The first Public Libraries Act was published in 1850, but Kensington Vestry was slow in adopting it. It was not until 1878 that a meeting of Kensington ratepayers, held at the Vestry Hall, determined that the Acts should be adopted. Kensington was not by then without a public library, but this had been provided by the generosity of James Heywood, a wealthy banker and local resident, and was not rate-maintained. It was not until 1888, however, that the Vestry's Libraries Commissioners decided that from a rateable income of about £3,300 three libraries could be maintained – at Notting Hill, Kensington and Brompton.

On 29 November, 1889 at 5.30 Her Royal Highness Princess Louise formally opened the Central Library in the old Vestry Hall on Kensington High Street. In 1960 this was moved to a new library on Hornton Street. Of particular note was the purpose-built Archive and Local Study area used to house the extensive collection of materials that had been built up since 1888.

104. *Before public libraries were common, and long after their appearance, circulating libraries catered for the mass demand for fiction at reasonable rates. Their bulk orders helped make the fortunes of such authors as Dickens and Thackeray. A circulating library is shown here at 25 Kensington High Street, c.1905.*

Jenny Lind

Known as the 'Swedish Nightingale', Jenny made her debut in 1838 as Agathe in Weber's *Der Freischütz*.

Jenny Lind (1820-1887) enjoyed living in Brompton. During her first visit to London in 1847 she stayed at Clareville Cottage on the Old Brompton Road and wrote to her mother on the delights of what was then a tranquil rural area. In 1876 she returned to the Old Brompton Road with her husband Otto Goldschmidt. Together they raised large sums of money for Brompton Hospital. Although Professor of Singing at the Royal College of Music she conducted many of her lessons from home. She was also an active member of the St Mary's, The Boltons, church choir.

105. *Jenny Lind in 1846. From the painting by Edward Magnus.*

There is a plaque commemorating her in **The Boltons** under the name Jenny Lind Goldschmidt.

Linley Sambourne House

Although outwardly indistinguishable from other classic Italianate houses in Kensington, 18 Stafford Terrace has been frozen in time. Home to *Punch* cartoonist Edward Linley Sambourne and his family, it is a unique example of a late Victorian town house with almost all of its furniture and fittings intact.

In 1874 Sambourne brought his young bride, Marion, to the house and the couple decided to furnish their home in the fashionable 'aesthetic' or artistic

106. *A room in Linley Sambourne House.*

107. *Linley Sambourne.*

style of the period. It became a focal point for many artists and writers such as Marcus Stone, Luke Fieldes, Herbert Beerbohm Tree, Rider Haggard and J M Barrie. Marion's diary provides a detailed account of life in Victorian Kensington, including menus and visitors.

Linley Sambourne worked for *Punch* for forty-three years and was still employed by the magazine when he died in 1910. He developed his own unique style. His cartoons were full of detail and to help with accuracy, he had a collection of 30,000 catalogued photographs, many taken by himself. He became a skilled and enthusiastic photographer and did his own developing in the top bathroom. Sambourne also worked as a book illustrator and is best known for work he did for Charles Kingsley's *Water Babies* and Hans Christian Andersen's *Fairy Tales*.

The Sambournes had two children, Roy who remained a bachelor, and Maud, who married Oliver Messel. The Messels' children, Oliver and Anne continued their parents' devotion to the house. Anne was first married to Ronald Armstrong Jones and their son Anthony married Princess Margaret. In 1980, Anne, then Countess of Rosse, sold the house to the Greater London Council and on the demise of that body it passed to the Royal Borough. It continued to be administered by the Victorian Society of which the Countess was a founder. For some years it has been open to the public complete with all its treasures.

In October 2000 the Victorian Society's lease was terminated – a decision agreed by all parties. The house was closed as part of the Royal Borough's conservation and development programme. Following two years of painstaking restoration and refurbishment of the whole house, new visitor facilities have been created in the base-ment, including an audio-visual film which introduces the Sambourne family and their extraordinary home.

Little Chelsea

Despite its name part of the isolated hamlet of Little Chelsea stretched over the Fulham Road into Kensington. In the late 17th century, the small settlement consisted mainly of fields and was cut off from the populated areas of Chelsea and Kensington.

Despite its remoteness, Little Chelsea had some distinguished residents. By 1700 it was the home of Anthony Ashley Cooper, 3rd Earl of Shaftesbury, who remained there until around 1706.

Fragmented in ownership and development, Little Chelsea evolved as a mix of villas, cottages, businesses, pubs, private madhouses and several schools. In the nineteenth century as building work gathered pace, the area began to lose its separateness and became part of the development of Fulham Road. **Lochee's Military Academy** was one of its most distinguished features.

The Llewelyn-Davies family

J M Barrie first met the Llewelyn Davies children in Kensington Gardens with their nanny Nancy Hodgson, while he was taking his daily walk with his St. Bernard, Porthos. To keep the boys in a perpetual state of amusement, he began to spin elaborate stories involving magical islands, Indians, pirates and fairies that enraptured the boys and ultimately inspired Barrie to write *Peter Pan*.

Barrie was soon introduced to their mother, the glamorous Sylvia du Maurier, daughter of renowned artist and novelist George du Maurier. Barrie wrote of Sylvia shortly after meeting her: "She is the most beautiful creature I have ever seen."

Barrie was so involved in the boys' lives that he even paid their private school tuition. Summers were spent at his country house at Black Lake, where he and the children played out elaborate pirate adventures that Barrie later recalled as the highlight of his life.

Unfortunately, in 1907, the boys' father Arthur died of cancer. Although Arthur had been suspicious of Barrie at first, the two men became very close at the end, and Barrie spent every day at Arthur's bedside, comforting the children and Sylvia. He also began to provide much of the family's financial support.

Then Sylvia too was afflicted with cancer, which she kept secret from the boys to spare them more pain. She died in 1910, six years after the premiere of *Peter Pan*. For Barrie, nothing was more devastating than watching his surrogate family fall apart.

Barrie became the unofficial guardian of the five Llewelyn Davies boys, then aged seven to seventeen. Though he provided for them handsomely and lavished them with attention, their lives as grown-ups were also fraught with tragedy. George, was killed in the trenches of the First World War; Michael, who hoped to be a writer, drowned at age 20 while studying at Oxford; and Peter committed suicide at the age of 63, many years after Barrie's death.

Lloyd-Webbers

The name of Lloyd-Webber is one which has become synonymous with music, Andrew as creator of musicals, and Julian as a classical cello soloist. Their popularity today should not, however, overshadow another Lloyd-Webber, their father, William. A brilliant musician in his own right he is still recalled with affection and respect at the Royal College of Music in Kensington where he worked as a professor for many years.

Similarly, Mrs Lloyd-Webber was music teacher at Wetherby School attended by both Andrew and Julian. The School later moved to Pembridge Square, where the Princes William and Harry attended. Julian still lives in South Kensington

Lochee's Military Academy

Lewis Lochee, who was born in Belgium, opened a military academy in **Little Chelsea** in 1770 in a large house at what is now 240-248 Fulham Road, opposite Chelsea and Westminster Hospital. An expert in fortification he wrote many books on the subject. One of the two known illustrations of the academy shows the frontage bristling with barricades and cannon. The other shows the ascent of a balloon from the roof in 1784. This was undertaken by Blanchard and Sheldon and watched by 'persons of fashion'. Many others must also have been present as locals complained of turnip fields being "despoiled by the multitude."

Lochee closed the academy in 1789 and the following year erected three houses, numbers 240-244 Fulham Road, at the corner of the site near Holly-

108. Lochee's Military Academy in Fulham Road.

wood Road. Lochee became a British citizen in 1781 but this did not prevent him from becoming involved in the Brabant revolt against the Austrian Government. He died in Lille in 1791.

London Academy of Music and Dramatic Arts

LAMDA was founded in 1861 with the aim of providing excellence in various musical disciplines as well as the performing arts. Providing instruction in spoken English, however, soon became a core area of the Academy's work. In the 1880s, it began offering speech examinations to the public and these have since been developed into the largest Speech and Drama Board in the UK.

Always based in West London, the Academy was forced to move to Hampton Court for a short time during the War after its studios were bombed. LAMDA then moved into Tower

110. Announcing the arrival of the new LAMDA theatre at Logan Place.

House in Earl's Court in 1946, where it stayed until 2005. It is now in larger premises in Talgarth Road. The Macowan Theatre in Logan Place, Earl's Court, was custom-built for the Academy and is still a major training ground. This theatre enables LAMDA to teach stage management and technical courses as well as providing a performance space.

Princess Louise

Princess Louise (1848-1939) was born at Buckingham Palace on March 18, 1848. She was the sixth of nine children of **Queen Victoria** and Prince Albert.

Edward Corbould, a professional artist of some note, was employed to teach the children art. Although the others were not without talent, Princess Louise had a natural aptitude and surpassed them all. At the age of twenty she attended the Kensington National Art Training School. She was an accomplished sculptor and Queen Victoria was persuaded to let Louise take lessons in sculpture from **Sir Joseph Boehm**, a relationship that was to cause much tabloid press speculation. Two of her sculptures can be seen locally, the statue of Queen Victoria in Kensington Gardens and a memorial to her brothers the Dukes of Edinburgh and Albany in St Mary Abbots Church.

Shortly after her marriage in 1871 to the Marquess of Lorne she moved into Kensington Palace which was to be her home for the rest of her life. Although they separated in 1880, she and her husband continued to live there. Louise became actively involved in charity work, including the Princess Louise Hospital for Children.

Edwin Lutyens

Sir Edwin Landseer Lutyens (1869-1944) is considered one of the greatest British architects of the 20th century. He designed many English country houses and was instrumental in the design and building of New Delhi. He was born in London and named after his father's friend,

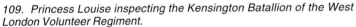

109. Princess Louise inspecting the Kensington Batallion of the West London Volunteer Regiment.

111. Sir Edwin Lutyens.

the painter and sculptor, Edwin Landseer. The family lived for many years in Onslow Square and he had a studio in Sydney Mews. Lutyens' first building in Kensington was Wetherby Studios. He also carried out several commissions including alterations for the writer Enid Bagnold at her Hyde Park Gate home. Sadly, there are no examples of his collaboration with the celebrated landscape designer Gertrude Jekyll in South Kensington.

Lutyens studied architecture at South Kensington School of Art from 1885 to 1887. After college he joined the **George and Peto** architectural practice. In 1924 he completed the supervision of the construction of what is perhaps his most popular design: Queen Mary's Dolls' House. Once displayed at Kensington Palace it is now a permanent exhibit in Windsor Castle. It was not conceived or built as a plaything for children but to showcase the finest British craftsmanship of the period.

Melton Court

It will come as no surprise to learn that Melton Court, opposite South Kensington Station, sits on nursery grounds, but this time two celebrated nurseries are involved.

Thomas Gibb, a seedsman from Somerset, established his five-acre nursery in 1800 both for horticultural purposes and for experiments to improve crop seeds. The nursery buildings were demolished in 1850 to make way for **Sir Charles Freake's** development of Onslow Crescent built between 1851 and 1861. Behind the crescent, Freake constructed a long glass conservatory for the florist and nurseryman, John Wills, with a shop entrance adjacent to Wills' house at number 16. In 1882 Wills, now recognised as a pioneer in floral decoration, entered into partnership with Samuel Segar. Their famous business continued to flourish, albeit in smaller premises, until the 1980s and the firm is still in business today at Canary Wharf.

When the **Smith's Charity Trustees** proposed the demolition of Onslow Crescent in 1935 it provoked an exchange of letters in *The Times*, mainly about the destruction of the garden enclosure, but to no avail. Melton Court an eight-storey block of flats with ground floor shops, was erected in 1936-38. The disputed garden enclosure was utilised by the Council to create the complex road junction between Old Brompton Road, Onslow Square and Pelham Street.

With the outbreak of war and a change in policy by the Smith's Charity Trustees, who now wished to preserve Freake's legacy, this mercifully was to be the last of the redevelopment plans.

Photographs in the Local Studies Library show the lower floors of Melton Court in use during the war as a munitions factory with women working for the war effort.

Freddie Mercury (1946-1991)

Freddie Mercury's house, 1 Logan Place, is surrounded by a high wall which is used by fans from all round the world to write messages. Although regularly cleaned, they quickly reappear.

While singing for Wreckage, a fellow student, Tim Staffell, introduced Freddie to Roger Taylor and Brian May, founder members of a band called *Smile*. After he finished his diploma in graphic art and design at Ealing, he joined a band called *Ibex*, taking over lead vocals from their guitarist. *Smile* metamorphosed into *Queen* when Freddie joined Roger and Brian to start a new band with himself as the lead vocalist. The final member of the band was bassist John Deacon. EMI Records promptly signed the band and in 1973 their debut album *Queen* was released and became iconic in rock history.

He was born Faroukh Bulsara in Zanzibar, and died Freddie Mercury with his friends by his side. On 24 November 1991, it was announced: "Freddie Mercury died peacefully this evening at his home at 1 Logan Place, Kensington. London. His death was the result of pneumonia brought on by AIDS."

Freddie was the first major rock star to die of the disease. During his last few months, he was cared for by a few very close friends, including his former girlfriend Mary Austen, with whom he remained close. In fact, it was Mary who inherited the Logan Place house, and still lives there today. Proposals to erect a statue of Freddie in Kensington were turned down by the Council – it now stands in Montreux, Switzerland

Merriman family

Kensington Square has always been popular with members of the medical profession. Richard Blackmore, physician to William III, was the first to arrive. Others included Sir John Simon, a pioneer in sanitary reform and pathologist who lived at no. 40 and Dr. James Veitch, the naval surgeon who revolutionised use of ligatures and introduced inoculation to the Navy at no. 33.

The most important medical residents though must be the Merriman family who lived at no. 45 for ninety years. They were John Merriman (1779-1839), his sons John junior and James Nathaniel and grandson John James, most of whom held the position of medical attendant to the Royal Family and Apothecary General to Queen Victoria.

Their house backed on to Young Street where John lived at no. 16 prior to moving into the Square and consulting rooms at no. 18. John Merriman junior was a keen historian and amateur photographer, in common with his near neighbour at no. 38 another doctor Arthur Roberts. Merriman left an important part of his collection of photographs, annotated books and records to the new Central Library which was, even in the early days, assiduously collecting items of local history.

Mews

A closer look at the history of the mews gives an insight into changing architectural styles, patterns of living, social class and urban development.

The word mews comes from

112. *Cornwall Mews South c.1970 – vital stables when they were built.*

the Royal Mews at Charing Cross, built on the site where the king's hawks were 'mewed'. This entailed keeping the birds in a cage or mew during moulting. During the reign of Henry VIII Royal Mews was converted into stables and thus the word came to mean stables grouped around a yard or alley. In the 18th century most property developments included a mews. These were entered through arches which helped to maintain the architectural integrity and were set a few feet lower than the surrounding properties to hide them from view. The most important part was the stabling for horses followed by basic accommodation for grooms and stable hands above.

They were hardly the most ideal environment to live in, often awash with manure and sewage with high levels of sickness and infant mortality, yet they existed side by side with those enjoying great wealth and luxury.

The arrival of railways signalled the beginning of the end for the mews as horses became somewhat redundant, and this was emphasised with the introduction of the car. Other uses had to be found for these premises. In 1908 the first mews was converted into residential accommodation. Others were used as garages and accommodation for chauffeurs or for servicing cars. Small industries, especially engineering ones, moved in. One such was George Rawlings, inventor of the **Rawlplug**, in Ashburn Mews. However, in one case a mews was retained as stabling. This was De Vere Mews which was until 1974 occupied by the Civil Service Riding Club. The horses were accommodated on the first floor, approached by a ramp.

Today mews properties are much sought after and command very high prices. Disadvantages of size and lack of windows are more than compensated by cobbled streets, unique architectural features and their secluded but central location.

Milestone Hotel

The Milestone Hotel is named after the old cast-iron milestone, which stands in its original position within the hotel's boundary. The house stood on part of the grounds previously occupied by the doomed mansion, Kensington House (*see Baron Grant*), and was erected in 1884. Among its more interesting occupants is the diplomat and author, the first Baron Redesdale (1837-1916), the grandfather of the famous Mitford sisters. In 1922 the house was converted into a hotel and later joined with 2 Kensington Court. John Athelstone Riley, grandson of the founder of the Union Bank,

113. John Stuart Mill by Spy.

114. John Everett Millais and his family; photograph by Lewis Carroll.

and the first occupant of no. 2 was largely responsible for the heavily ornamented exterior and lavishly decorated interior.

In August 1986, the Milestone was badly damaged in a fire. The blaze took three hours to control and the reason for the fire remains a mystery. The hotel deteriorated further until it was sold to Red Carnation Hotels who restored its architectural splendour. Today, the Milestone has been recognised with numerous awards and accolades and ranks as one of the best hotels in the world.

John Stuart Mill

Born and raised in Kensington Church Street, John Stuart Mill (1806-1873) moved with his mother and sister to 18 Kensington Square in 1837 after his father's death. He was a great philosopher, friend of Jeremy Bentham and founder of 'Utilitarianism' – the promotion of the greatest happiness of the greatest number. Mill's famous

System of Logic was written whilst he lived there, but the house is best known for the literary calamity that happened in 1835. Carlyle's manuscript (the only copy) of the first volume of his *History of the French Revolution* was inadvertently burnt by a maid who mistook the scattered papers for kindling. Mill had to take a cab to Carlyle's home in Chelsea and tell him what had happened and offered £100 as compensation.

Mill also supported the members of the **Kensington Society** who were fighting for the emancipation of women. How appropriate that his house was for many years the home of Gay Christiansen, founder of the present Kensington Society.

John Everett Millais

When the **Duke of Sussex** presented the prizes at the Bloomsbury School of Art in 1839, Mr Millais was called out as the winner of the Royal Society of Arts Silver Medal and a small boy in a pinafore came forward to receive the award. This was the ten-year-old Millais (1829-1896). The following year he was admitted to the Royal Academy School where he continued to win prize after prize, culminating in the Gold Medal in 1847. The following year he became a founder member of the Pre-Raphaelite Brotherhood.

Admired by Ruskin, the two toured together in Scotland, during which time Millais and Ruskin's wife, Effie, fell in love.

Ruskin and Effie divorced and she married Millais in 1855. They had eight children.

Millais moved to 7 Cromwell Place to join the London High Society set. Here he rejected Pre-Raphaelite ideals by copying the styles of the grandmasters and encouraged others to do the same. His successes allowed him to build a grand new house at 2 Palace Gate which was so extravagant that Thomas Carlyle stated, while sitting for his portrait, "Millais, did painting do all that? ... Well, there must be more fools in this world than I had thought!"

During his life, Millais' success never waned. In 1885 he became a baronet and in 1896 succeeded Leighton as President of the Royal Academy, an office he held for less than six months as he died at home that year of cancer.

Motor Industry

It is surprising that much of the early development of the British motor industry took place in Kensington. All over South Kensington engineers were setting up small workshops to develop spare parts or to service cars. **Mews**, no longer required for stabling, were quickly adapted for use as garages. Athelstone Mews is a good example. George Debnam took over the lease in 1917 and soon was holding the Daimler franchise in London. Employees were also involved in the early days of motor racing, often with some success.

In 1913 Robert Bamford and Lionel Martin bought premises in Henniker Mews and the following March, the very first Aston Martin car was registered. Fitted with a Coventry Simplex side-valve engine, and built to their own specification, it became known as the 'Coal Scuttle'. By 1920 the company was operating from 53 Abingdon Road.

Century Motors Ltd took over a carriage manufacturers on Kensington High Street. At the rear there was space for 150 cars. Advertisements for Astahl Touring Cars, Berna Commercial Motors and Aster chassis and spares were displayed on the forecourt. The site was to become an aircraft factory and an amusement park before its final use as a Post Office.

Empire House and Michelin House are the great lasting legacies of these exciting early years of the motor car. Continental Tyres of America and Michelin of France continued their battle for supremacy in tyre manufacture in the Fulham Road. The striking art nouveau Michelin House was the first to be built in 1909 soon followed by Empire House at the junction of the then Fulham and Brompton Roads.

Murderers

Throughout the ages nefarious activities have been conducted behind the respectable façades of Kensington houses. However, it still comes as a surprise to discover that some of England's most infamous murders took place in the area.

John Haigh, the acid bath murderer, rented a basement at 79 Gloucester Road to make plastic fingernails, a job apparently requiring a bath containing prussic acid. In 1944 he shot Donald McSwann and dissolved his body in this bath. Ten months later he did the same to Donald's parents when they came to look for their son. Using a forged power of attorney he then sold their effects. While staying at the Onslow Court Hotel, now Jury's in Queen's Gate, Haigh met Olivia Durand-Deacon in the bar and invited her to see how he made fingernails. This time he drove to Crawley were he had another 'bath'. On his arrest he was nicknamed the 'Vampire of Kensington' by the press and later confessed to nine murders. He was hanged in 1949.

On her first day as manageress of the Knightsbridge Little Club, a drinking place in the Brompton Road, Ruth Ellis met the debonair amateur racing driver David Blakely. Within a very short time she moved into a bed-sitter at 44 Egerton Gardens provided by him. The relationship was tempestuous, fuelled by her jealousy and Blakely's violent temper. On the night of 9 April 1955 they went to a film and then back to Egerton Gardens. The next day she asked a former boyfriend to take her to the Magdala public house in Hampstead where she shot Blakely dead. Ruth was arrested with the smoking gun still in her hands and her trial opened in June 1955. She was found guilty by the jury in 14 minutes and Mr Justice Havers sentenced her to death. On 13 July 1955 she became the last woman to be executed in Britain. In February 2002 an appeal was launched to change the charge to manslaughter on the grounds of diminished responsibility. The appeal was rejected as this defence was not introduced until 1957.

Colin Ireland, a serial killer, made his first kill in 1993 when he picked up Peter Walker a 45-year-old choreographer at the

115. The Natural History Museum at the beginning of the 20th century.

Coleherne pub in the Old Brompton Road. They made their way back to Walker's flat in Battersea, where Ireland killed him. Walker's body was soon discovered, but the police had nothing to go on. Ireland had cleverly covered his tracks.

After just over two months, he returned to the Coleherne on 28 May. His second victim was thirty-seven-year-old librarian Christopher Dunn. Dunn's body was discovered by a friend two days later. On 4 June, just six days after he murdered Christopher Dunn, he killed an American, thirty-five-year-old Perry Bradley III. Angered by the lack of publicity despite committing three murders, Ireland killed Andrew Collier three days later, this time leaving a clue for the police. Ireland's fifth and final

victim was 41-year-old Emanuel Spiteri, a Maltese chef. All his victims were picked up at the Coleherne.

On 19 July, Ireland walked into his solicitor's office in South-end-on-Sea in Essex, and told him that he had been with Spiteri that night but claimed he was not the killer. However he was charged with Collier's murder on 21 July, with Spiteri's two days later and in August he confessed to all five murders.

When six terrorists seized the Iranian Embassy in Princes Gate on 30 April 1980 viewers in their millions turned on their televisions to watch the unfolding drama and the dramatic rescue by the SAS. One lesser known fact is that the terrorists planned the attack in a flat in Lexham Gardens.

Natural History Museum

One of the most notable and instantly recognisable buildings in London, the Natural History Museum, designed by Sir Alfred Waterhouse, was opened to the public in 1881. However, its origins go back more than 250 years.

It all started when physician and collector of natural curiosities, Sir Hans Sloane, who lived in Chelsea, left his extensive collection to the nation in 1753 at a bargain price. As the natural collections grew there was insufficient space at the British Museum to store and display them. Sir Richard Owen was the main force behind a move to a new site; he had many new ideas for displays and was eager to have the space to carry out his plans.

The 1851 Commissioners offered the site previously occupied by the 1862 International Exhibition building, once described as 'the ugliest building in London'. Ironically, it was the architect of that building, Captain **Francis Fowke**, who won the design competition for the new Natural History Museum.

However, in 1865 Fowke died suddenly and the contract was awarded instead to a rising young architect from Manchester, Alfred Waterhouse, who altered Fowke's design from Renaissance to German Romanesque, creating the beautiful Waterhouse Building we know today. The key features are the terracotta walls, the carved animals and plants that decorate every corner inside and out, the magnificent entrance and of course the vast Central Hall. By 1883 the mineralogy and natural history items were in their new home, but the collections were not finally declared a museum in their own right until 1963.

Recently all the galleries have been extensively refurbished and brought up to date. More natural scenarios and interactive features have replaced the endless rows of stuffed animals. One feature will never change; the dinosaur skeleton in the Central Hall. New blocks, such as the Earth Galleries, have been added and the latest addition is the Darwin Centre. This houses the museum's vast collection of bottled specimens and is the research centre. The grounds are also used for major London events such as Fashion Week and at Christmas for a skating rink.

Northcliffe House

As the printing presses in Fleet Street fell silent, newspapers moved to alternative premises in London. The Daily Mail and General Trust plc, incorporated in 1922, moved to Northcliffe House at no 2 Derry Street in 1988, a building named after the press baron, Alfred Harmsworth, Baron Northcliffe (1865-1922), owner of *The Times* and founder of the *Daily Mail*.

When it became clear that **Barker's** sale area was too large for modern trade, the number of sales floors was reduced to four and the remainder converted into office space. 10,000 tons of rubble was removed from the rear of the store to create a vast 115-foot high barrel vaulted atrium, with a domed roof containing 64 tons of glass overlooking garden terraces. This spectacular atrium, the largest in Europe, is the entrance hall to Northcliffe House. It is here that the *Daily Mail*, the *Evening Standard* and *Metro* are published. An extra floor of office space was acquired when Barker's closed its doors in January 2006.

Michael Novosielski

Novosielski (1750-1795), a Roman born architect of Polish descent, borrowed money to erect a terrace of forty dwellings fronting onto the Brompton Road, west of Yeoman's Row. These he dubbed 'Michael's Place'. They were decent enough to attract the singer Elizabeth Billington to live at no. 16 between 1792 and 1793, whilst **William Cobbett** lived at no 11 in 1820-1821. '

Novosielski also built a large house for himself, Brompton Grange at the southern end of **Yeoman's Row** in 1787. This was sold to John Willet Payne, a sailor noted for reckless gallantry in combat and reckless dissipation off duty. From 1830 the celebrated singer John Braham lived there. Brompton Grange was then demolished to make way for the construction of Egerton Terrace, Crescent and Place. Novosielski's other houses were finally knocked down in the 1880s to be replaced by shops and houses.

Nurseries

The land use maps produced by Milne in the 1800s show southern Kensington almost entirely occupied by market gardens and nurseries from Brompton to Earls Court. The market gardens supplied London with fresh produce along roads into the West End which were described as "frequently congested with the carriage of produce from market gardens and heavy return loads of manure". Forty years later the 1843 Tithe maps show that 57% of southern Kensington was still under cultivation.

Many nurseries achieved national and international reputations. The most famous was **Brompton Park**, closely followed by **Furber's Nursery** sited between Victoria Road and Gloucester Road. Others included Harrison's Nursery, which was based in South Kensington and Selwood's opposite the Queen's Elm where Rugergall grew the first lettuces in England and which was later occupied by William Curtis,

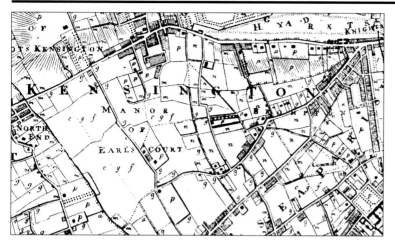

116. A land use map by Thomas Milne c.1800, which shows the open fields of Kensington.

118. William Curtis, botanist.

117. Malcolm's Nursery in Kensington Road. The De Vere Hotel is now on the site. Watercolour.

author of *Flora Londinensis* and founder of the *Botanical Magazine*.

These enterprises were very innovative and highly successful. They generated handsome profits to local landowners; it was only when speculative building became even more profitable in the mid 19th century that nurseries finally succumbed to the unstoppable spread of bricks and mortar.

The Odeon

The Kensington Kinema, which prided itself as the largest in the country, was opened in 1926 with seating for 2,500 people. It was designed by Julian Rudolph Leathart and famed for its fabulous interior which included a restaurant and billiard saloon Its name was changed to the Majestic, then to the Kensington, and is now the Odeon.

Odeon cinemas were created in the 1930s by Oscar Deutsch.

'Odeon' was possibly derived from his motto, "**O**scar **D**eutsch **E**ntertains **O**ur **N**ation". The Odeons had a different character to most other cinemas in the UK, often having unique and spectacular interiors. Many have sadly disappeared, or often reduced to banal multiplexes with small screens. The one at Kensington now has six screens.

Minerva and residential specialists Northacre have recently purchased the Odeon for an estimated £24 million. They plan to redevelop the site as a new multi-screen with flats on the upper floors and behind together with underground parking. The planning application is being strongly opposed by the Cinema Theatre Association and local residents led by film director, Michael Winner. To date attempts to have the cinema listed have failed. It is argued that as the interiors have been ripped out there is no longer a case for conservation; supporters argue that some of the original features remain behind false walls. It will be interesting to see who wins the fight.

119. *An elephant from a local circus promoting National Savings, walking past Kensington Odeon in the 1950s.*

Our Lady of Victories

In 1813 the first Roman Catholic chapel since the Reformation was established in Holland Street and dedicated to St Mary. By 1850 St Mary's took the role of parish church under the direction of Father James Foley. Encouraged by the growing congregation and the opening of the Carmelite Church on Church Street, Father Foley purchased for £5000 a plot on the south side of Kensington High Street, near the junction with Earl's Court Road.

The designs for Our Lady of Victories by George Goldie and based on the Gothic style of 13th-century France, had a mixed reception. A major problem was the narrow entrance to the High Street, barely thirty feet wide, which meant the church was almost completely hidden. The present Gothic arch entrance was not built until 1935 when the church acquired additional frontage. It was elevated to the status of a Pro-Cathedral in 1865, which it held until West-

120. *The interior of Our Lady of Victories, c.1896.*

Mervyn Lawrence Peake

Son of missionaries, Mervyn Peake (1911-1968) was born in Southern China. Educated in Tientsin Grammar School he attended Eltham College and the Royal Academy Schools after returning to England. Failing his exams he travelled to Sark in 1933 to join an artist commune, returning to London in 1935. He married Maeve Gilmore in 1937 and they had three children.

In 1935 Peake taught life drawing at Westminster School of Art, exhibiting in 1938. He quit in 1939, launched a joint exhibition with Maeve and published his illustrated children's book *Captain Slaughter-board drops Anchor*. Both his artworks and writing achieved critical praise. His illustrations for *Rime of the Ancient Mariner* were widely admired, as were his pictures for *Ride-a-Cock-Horse and other Nursery Rhymes*. His greatest novel was his surreal fantasy *Gormenghast*, recently dramatized by the BBC. Other works include his drawing manuals, poems and plays.

After a breakdown in 1957 Peake contracted Parkinson's disease. On his arrival at Drayton Gardens in 1960 he was largely incapacitated. Only able to work in short bursts he still managed to write *Titus Awakes* and illustrate his poem *The Rhyme of the Flying Bomb*. He died at a home in Berkshire.

Pettit's, drapers

One business resisted the blandishments of **Barkers'** expansionism and that was Pettit's, drapers and outfitters. The shop

121. Mervyn Peake in 1946.

minster Cathedral opened in 1903.

In 1940 the church was destroyed by enemy action and for seventeen years the congregation had to worship in temporary surroundings. First in the nearby **Odeon**, then at a rent of one shilling a year at the Cavendish Furniture Showrooms, then until recently Safeways (later Somerfields) supermarket, and finally at the Kensington Chapel, Allen Street.

Trees twenty feet high were growing in the nave before rebuilding began to the designs of Sir Adrian Gilbert Scott. The new church was consecrated in 1959.

was opened by William Pettit on the corner of Allen Street and the High Street in 1886. They survived almost long enough to celebrate their centenary, but rising postal costs seriously affected its large mail order business.

It was a small shop, devoted to women's clothing. Some of the goods were of high quality but rather old-fashioned in style. For instance, there was a large corsetry department, selling lace-up corsets of the type worn by women born around 1900. Pettit's also sold serviceable woollen skirts, and the good suits 'suitable for country wear'. These were made to last. Changing fashions contributed to the firm's demise in 1977.

Photographers

It is through the photographer's art that we can gain a much clearer idea of how Kensington has changed over the past 150 years. Images by both professional and amateurs have captured people, places and events that have shaped the area from the 1860s up to today. Argent Archer and H R Stiles both had studios on the High Street and faithfully recorded changes between the 1880s and 1930s. Many of their now very fragile glass plates are kept in the Local Studies Library and examples can be found in this book. Ernest Milner, in the first decade of the 20th century, compiled a photographic record of every property along the route of the Piccadilly line, including every shop front on the Brompton Road. Notable amateurs include John **Merriman** and Arthur Roberts, both physicians, who took some of the earliest photographs, mainly in the 1860s, of the old High Street, St Mary Ab-

122. Argent Archer's Studio on Kensington High Street near the junction with Campden Hill Road, now Phillimore Court, c.1895.

bots and Earl's Court Farm. Rupert Potter, **Beatrix Potter's** father, was also a keen amateur photographer working mainly in South Kensington.

Linley Sambourne was another keen amateur photographer. As well as the pictures he took to assist his work as a cartoonist, he also photographed local scenes. He developed a special 'spy' camera to capture passers-by without them knowing.

Several society photographers were based in Kensington. Royal photographer, Cecil Beaton, lived at 8 Pelham Place where he entertained notable names including the Queen Mother. Portrait photographer,

Godfrey Argent, owned two studios in the Borough, first at Queen's Gate and then Holland Street. In the 1960s he became a Royal photographer and in 1967 was appointed official photographer for the National Photographic Record, based at the National Portrait Gallery. This came about through his purchase of Walter Bird's archive containing over 5,000 photographs taken for the project since 1917 and Sir Roy Strong encouraged him to extend the record beyond the traditional subjects to include cultural figures such as Noel Coward, David Hockney and Philip Larkin. Argent died in June 2006.

123. *Augustus Pitt-Rivers.*

Augustus Pitt-Rivers

Augustus Henry Lane Pitt-Rivers (1827-1900) lived in some opulence at 19/21 Penywern Road from 1878 to 1881, years which marked a crucial turning-point in his life. The census shows he had no less than eleven servants. Pitt-Rivers was known as Augustus Lane Fox until changing his name to Pitt Rivers in the course of inheriting a 27,000 acre estate at Cranborne Chase, Dorset from his great uncle in 1880.

The estate was to prove rich in archaeological remains ranging across Roman and Saxon periods. He threw himself into systematically excavating and recording digs on his land. It was only natural that Pitt-Rivers should become the country's first inspector of ancient monuments, after the passing of Sir John Lubbock's Ancient Monuments Act in 1882. Lubbock would later become his son-in-law.

The Pitt Rivers Museum in Oxford was founded in 1884

when he gave his vast archaeological collection to the University. His two conditions were that a museum was built to house it and that someone should be appointed to lecture in anthropology. However, most of the excavated material from Cranborne Chase is held at the Salisbury and South Wiltshire Museum, where a gallery is devoted to Pitt-Rivers and his work.

Pontings

"The largest fancy goods and silk business in London" was set up by the Ponting Brothers on a site between the station and Wrights Lane in the 1870s. In 1893 the then derelict **Scarsdale House** was added, initially as housing for staff. Following the death of William Ponting the ramshackle but successful old shop was changed into a handsome emporium. As the costs multiplied, in particular the expansion into the newly erected station arcade, debts mounted and in 1906 they went into liquidation.

Eagerly snapped up by **Barker's**, largely through Sydney

Skinner's influence, for £84,000 it continued to run as an outwardly independent concern. Following the takeover of Derry & Toms renovations were carried out to the whole block, including new display windows and a big clock bearing the slogan "Pontings – the House for Value."

A mail order department and loading block to meet the demands of an ever expanding trade was set up in Scarsdale Terrace which was to continue until the 1960s; the building was later known as College House. The rest of the store was less successful except at sales times when Pontings' Bargain Basement was a key attraction. Special trains were run to Kensington to bring customers to the three stores now under the Barker's umbrella.

In 1970 as part of a rationalization carried out by the House of Fraser, now parent company of the old Barker's group, Pontings was closed. The entire contents were moved within forty hours and installed in the lower ground floor of the Barker's building where it continued as 'Pontings Bargain Basement'.

124. *Pontings on Kensington High Street, at the junction with Wright's Lane, 1961.*

The Pontings building was briefly taken over by a market known as Kensington Super Store but the site was redeveloped by the English Property Corporation who built office blocks, luxury flats and shops.

Beatrix Potter

Without doubt one of the saddest but possibly the best known Brompton resident was Beatrix Potter (1866-1943). Born at 2, Bolton Gardens, this was to be her home until 1913. The Potter family made their fortune in the Lancashire textile industry thus Rupert, Beatrix's father, was able to live a life of independent means as a gentleman.

Beatrix lived a very restricted life, as she was neither allowed to go to school nor have any friends as her mother felt she was too delicate. A very solitary child she spent her days reading and studying enlivened by the occasional visit to the South Kensington museums, only seeing her parents at bedtime and on special occasions. Her brother Bertram was born when she was six but was soon sent away to school. From an early age she kept a diary, written in code and illustrated with little drawings. Not surprisingly, it was her governess who recognised and encouraged her talent. She also colluded with the smuggling of small animals back to the London house after the Easter and summer holidays. These included snails in a plant pot, a rabbit and a hedgehog. Soon children everywhere were to know about her pets. Peter Rabbit was written in 1900, followed by Squirrel Nutkin in 1903 and Benjamin Bunny in 1904.

Aged 19 she wrote "extraor-

125. Beatrix Potter, outside the door of 2 Bolton Gardens.

dinary to state that this is the first time in my life that I have been to Horse Guards, the Admiralty or seen the Strand or Monument". Her parents, both crashing snobs, continued to interfere in all her relationships and refused to allow her to marry her publisher Norman Warne because he was 'in trade'. Eventually aged 47 she married her solicitor William Heelis in 1913 and finally escaped from Bolton Gardens. The house was destroyed in the Second World War and is now the site of **Bousfield School.**

Princess Beatrice Hospital

Opened in 1887 as a 'Jubilee Hospital' as part of Queen Victoria's 50-year anniversary celebrations, it was a voluntary hospital mainly for the poor. Between 1907 and 1931 it became a general hospital for Kensington, Chelsea and Fulham. The new Princess Beatrice hospital

was opened in 1932 with the foundation stone laid by Princess Beatrice in 1930, hence the change of name. Princess Beatrice born in 1857 was the youngest of Victoria and Albert's nine children.

In 1948 the hospital became part of the National Health Service and was designated a teaching hospital linked to St George's. Houses in Finborough Road were then taken over as residences for trainee nurses. Later it specialised in obstetrics.

All the hospital scenes in the 1981 hit film *American Werewolf in London* were shot here, and Jenny Agutter's flat, where the transformation scenes were shot, was located close by in Redcliffe Gardens. The hospital closed in 1978 and converted into a hostel called Princess Beatrice House in 1985. The hostel is now run by Look Ahead which helps to provide vulnerable people with a home and support to enable them in the future to lead independent lives.

Queen's Gate

South Kensington's grand boulevard, Queen's Gate, was created in the 1850s through the co-operation of the **1851 Commissioners**, H B Alexander and the 5th Earl of Harrington with the southern section added by **Sir Charles Freake** in the 1870s. Originally called Prince Albert's Road, building began with nos. 5-19 in 1855 and completed with no.184 in 1895. All of the most important Victorian architects and builders were involved including C J Richardson, Thomas Cundy III, Charles Aldin, Sir Charles Freake and Norman Shaw.

Despite the involvement of so

126. *Queen's Gate, c. 1905, looking north from the junction with Harrington Road. Queen's Gate school, at nos. 131-133, is located in the lighter coloured houses in the centre right.*

many people the houses are remarkably similar in design, Italianate white or cream stucco. The exception being the north-east part where red brick Queen Anne style houses predominate, some of which were refaced to meet the changing fashion. But the demand for five-storey palatial family houses was falling off and by the late 1870s many remained unoccupied. Thus began the conversion into flats, hotels, embassies and schools.

Baden Powell House, headquarters of the Scouts' Association, was built in 1961 at the junction with Cromwell Road. It also houses a museum housing Baden Powell archives and memorabilia including a loaf of bread baked during the siege of Mafeking in 1899.

The statue of Lord Napier of Magdala by **Sir Joseph Boehm** standing at the north end of Queen's Gate was moved here in 1921. His mount stands on an upward slope to fit in with the gradient of its original site in Waterloo Place.

Queen's Gate School

Miss Eleanor Beatrice Wyatt was the first to take one of the **Queen's Gate** properties for a school. In 1891 she moved to no. 132 from Stanhope Gardens so as to meet the demand for places for girls including boarders, known as House Girls. Within a few years no. 133 was added. In 1899 Miss Wyatt acquired Heathfield in Ascot and moved there with most of the House Girls. The Kensington school was then passed over to Miss Douglas with only 32 on the roll. Places were soon filled and more property acquired in the mews behind. Unusually for a school of this type the girls did not wear a uniform, which is still the case today.

In 1919 Miss Hilda Spalding took over and it became known as 'Spee's' and was primarily a finishing school. No. 131 was acquired to house the now expanding junior school. During the war the school was evacuated to Downe House in Newbury and the Queen's Gate houses were used by the London Auxiliary Fire Brigade. Much work was needed to restore the damaged building after the war but life soon returned to normal.

Mrs Margaret See took over in the 1950s and during her time the school grew from strength to strength. She was to introduce a more academic approach. The number of girls doing A-levels greatly increased, even the finishing girls had to take at least one public exam. Both the author

Penelope Fitzgerald and Elizabeth Manningham-Buller, Director General of MI5 taught at the school. Famous pupils include Vanessa and Lynn Redgrave, Lucinda Lambton, Nigella Lawson and Trinny (Woodall) and Susannah (Constantine). But perhaps the best known is Camilla Shand, now Duchess of Cornwall, who was a House Girl.

In 2006 nos. 125 and 126, formerly a hostel belonging to the Girls' Friendly Society, were purchased. These will house the Junior School, new science labs and a drama suite.

Peggy Ramsay

Peggy Ramsay (1908-1991) was one of the best-known playwrights' agents in the country. She established her agency in 1953 and it continued until her death in 1991. Her client list was a veritable *Who's Who* of the theatrical world and included Alan Ayckbourn, Robert Bolt, David Hare, Eugene Ionesco, Joe Orton, Stephen Poliakoff and J B Priestley.

Her influence was such that when she died, bequeathing her papers to the British Library, they were judged significant enough for a selection to be exhibited in their own showcase in the King's Library. Peggy, who lived in a basement flat in Redcliffe Square, gained a wider posthumous fame as the subject of *Love is Where it Falls*, Simon Callow's account of their passionate but platonic relationship.

When she died her estate amounted to some £1.5 million and was left to help writers and writing for the stage with especial reference to her friends and clients. Her executors are

127. Terence Rattigan during the time of the production of The Browning Version.

Laurence Harbottle and Simon Callow who established the Peggy Ramsay Foundation.

Terence Rattigan

Terence Mervyn Rattigan (1911-1977) was one of England's most important and prolific 20th-century dramatists. He was born at 100 Cornwall Gardens and it was there that he spent much of his childhood. It was called Lanarkslea and was the home of his grandfather, a chief justice of the Punjab. It was while living there that the young Terence was first taken to the theatre and by 1918, at the age of just seven, he declared his intention of becoming a playwright.

Success came early, with the light comedy *French Without Tears* in 1936. Rattigan's determination to write a more serious play produced *After the Dance* 1939. Unfortunately the war defeated the play's chances of a long run. Rattigan alternated between comedies and dramas, and after the war, a string of

dramas made his name: *The Winslow Boy* (1946), *The Browning Version* (1948), *The Deep Blue Sea* (1952), and *Separate Tables* (1954).

Rattigan was commemorated with an English Heritage Blue Plaque in 2005, unveiled by David Suchet who played in the West End production of Rattigan's *Man and Boy*. Actors Patricia Hodge, Penelope Wilton, Ian Holme, Stephen Fry and Julian Glover also attended.

Rawlplugs

Rawlplugs were developed in Rawlings Bros garage in Ashburn Mews. George Rawlings was involved in making electrical wall fittings for the British Museum and in 1919 developed his fibre plug as the least destructive way of making a firm fixing. As the company, now called Rawlplug Company Ltd, became more successful they moved to 87a and 89 Cromwell Road and by 1939 had become a global business. In the 1960s additional properties were acquired for more office space, but when planning permission was refused the company moved out to Kingston in 1966.

Roof Garden

High above street level outside the old **Derry & Toms** building a glimpse of foliage can be seen, a hint of the delights of the famous Kensington Roof Garden. **Trevor Bowen** wanted to create the most impressive tea room and restaurant in London. Ralph Handcock was commissioned to lay out the gardens working under the supervision of the store's architect Bernard George, who designed

128. The Roof Garden of Derry and Toms store, showing Bernard George's Sun Pavilion. Watercolour by Joseph Pike.

the Sun Pavilion, formerly the centre piece of the garden.

Completed in 1938, it was opened by the Earl of Athlone. It cost £25,000 and consisted of three areas, an English Garden, a Tudor Court and a Moorish garden with fountains, all divided by arches and follies. Its remarkable construction, a bed of brick and rubble on a bitumen base, allows for the shallowest possible soil, yet it supports full grown trees, flower beds, a small stream and a pond, complete with ducks and flamingos. Despite being on a rooftop, the trees were made the subject of tree preservation orders in 1976. The gardens, situated 30 metres above street level, provide a panoramic view over west London on a clear day.

In its brief pre-war life it was opened daily and many chari-table events were held attended by well known personalities and Royalty. During the war a bomb hit the garden but passed through exploding on the fourth floor. Following the sale to the House of Fraser the Roof Garden was leased for use as a restau-rant and nightclub and is cur-rently held by Richard Branson.

The Royal Borough

On 20 November 1901 a Royal Charter granted Kensington the title Royal Borough of Kensing-ton. Earlier in May the Home Secretary wrote to the Mayor announcing that he was "com-manded by His Majesty to inform you that in accordance with the expressed wish of Her Late Maj-esty that her birth place at Ken-sington Palace should be so com-memorated, His Majesty has been graciously pleased to command that the Borough should in fu-ture be designated The Royal Borough of Kensington.

With the amalgamation of the Kensington and Chelsea bor-oughs, Queen Elizabeth II ex-tended the use of the Royal title to the new Borough. This was highly appropriate in view of Chelsea's long association with Royalty starting with King Henry VIII's purchase of the Manor of Chelsea in 1536.

The title does not carry any special rights or privileges but is seen as an honour and a mat-ter of civic pride. There are only two other Royal Boroughs in the country namely Windsor and Maidenhead and Kingston-upon-Thames.

Royal British Society of Sculptors

The Royal British Society of Sculptors is based at 108 Old Brompton Road. Founded in 1904 it is a membership society for professional sculptors. First granted in 1911, royal patronage continues today with HM Queen Elizabeth II. Leading sculptors involved over the years include Sir Hamo Thorneycroft, Alfred Gilbert, Ivor Roberts-Jones, Dame Elisabeth Frink, Michael Kenny, Sir Anthony Caro, Eduardo Chillida, Richard Serra, Philip King, Allen Jones, Michael Sandle and many others.

Exhibition space is provided for members and there is an exciting range of talks, educa-tional courses and workshops. There is also an archive with material covering over 100 years of British sculpture. Today, the em-phasis is on contemporary sculpture and education.

Royal College of Organists

The College was established in 1864 through the energies of Richard Limpus, who was a former organist of St Michael's, Cornhill in the City of London.

In 1904 the College moved into the building that once housed the National Training School for Music, which was erected by **Charles Freake** at his own cost. The School opened in 1876 with **Arthur Sullivan** as its first Principal. Designed by Henry Cole's eldest son, Lt. H Cole who gave his services free, the frontage was decorated with sgriaffito work designed and executed by staff and pupils at the National Art Training School. The building soon proved to be too small and a new building, the Royal College of Music, was commissioned in Prince Consort Road. For several years the building remained empty until the Organists moved in in 1904.

In 1990 because of increased costs the College was forced to leave the premises. At present, although a viable organisation, they do not have premises.

The Royal Commission for the Exhibition of 1851

Many people are surprised to learn that this august body, established by Queen Victoria in 1850 to mastermind the Great Exhibition, is still active. Moreover, it continues to fulfil Prince Albert's vision by sponsoring the development of science and technology and its application to industry. In 1850 Prince Albert was appointed President;

129. The Royal College of Organists, 1905.

today that role is taken by Prince Philip.

When the Great Exhibition closed the Commission was expected to be dissolved but instead was given a Royal Charter so that it could administer the substantial profits for charitable purposes. The charter charged the Commission with "increasing the means of industrial education and extending the influence of science and art upon productive industry". To fulfil this they purchased 86 acres of land in South Kensington to build a cultural and educational centre. Some of the estate was leased to property speculators and the money raised used to build the world renowned South Kensington museums and institutions of learning.

The Commission continued to own the freehold of, and manage much of this estate and as this huge undertaking neared completion other uses for the funds were sought. In 1891 an educational trust was set up to perpetuate its aims. Today, with assets of over £30 million, fellowships and grants totalling over £1 million are disbursed annually for those involved in pure scientific research and engineering and those involved with its application to industry.

Many outstanding scientists and engineers have received research grants, including eleven Nobel Laureates, four Presidents and 130 Fellows of the Royal Society.

130. *The Royal Commissioners for the 1851 Exhibition, painting by H W Phillips. The Commissioners are, left to right; Standing: C W Dilke, John Scott Russell, Henry Cole, Charles Fox, Joseph Paxton, Lord John Russell, Sir Robert Peel, Robert Stephenson; Seated: Richard Cobden, Charles Barry, Lord Grenville, William Cubitt, Prince Albert, Lord Derby. In fact the artist of this contrived picture was inaccurate, since Paxton and Fox were not members of the Commission.*

Royal Horticultural Society Gardens

An attraction in **Albertopolis** was the show garden of the Royal Horticultural Society which was opened by Prince Albert in 1861. Many of the buildings were designed by **Francis Fowke** including an immense conservatory cast in iron, a great staircase leading to a terrace walk lit by gas lighting, elegant bandstands and water features.

The Prince saw the garden as a way of attracting the public to the science and art of gardening with the skills of sculpture, painting and architecture, as well as horticulture, on display. However, the RHS had more exclusive ideas and did little to encourage the general public. Indeed they feared that the 1862 Exhibition being planned next door, would threaten their privacy, and that they might be "subjected to disagreeable annoyance and comment from the windows of the refreshment room".

The site, so near to London, was not ideal, as smoke pollution had an adverse effect on cultivation. In 1876 the Society surrendered its lease to the Commissioners who had plans to build a **Science Museum** on much of the site.

131. *The Royal Horticultural Society Gardens at Kensington. View from the International Exhibition in 1862.*

132. Programme of the Royal Kent Theatre, July 1831.

Royal Kent Theatre

This is one of the lost London theatres. Kensington's only theatre closed after a very short and chequered career. It was situated in a narrow street off Kensington High Street known as Brown's Buildings – the site is now covered by Kensington Fire Station in Old Court Place. Known first as the Royal Kensington Theatre, the building was small, accommodating only about 300. The venture began as a subscription club theatre as it had been unable to get a public licence. When this was eventually obtained, with the support of the Duchess of Kent, the name was changed in her honour.

The first production on 31 July 1831 was *Othello* and this was repeated when it reopened after a long closure in 1834. Productions during its seventeen years included classics such as *The Beggar's Opera* and *She Stoops to Conquer*.

The theatre usually opened at 6.30 pm, the fashionable time in those days, but there was also admission for latecomers at reduced prices at 8.30pm. The programme was arranged so that the audience saw at least one of the plays but unfortunately many were too drunk to appreciate them.

In 1838, there was a balloon ascent from the theatre's roof. The Royal Kent, however, was plagued with failures and disturbances including a riot, when being unpaid, the cast decamped after the first act one evening with the takings. The furious audience stormed the stage, broke up the seats and smashed the windows. When it re-opened in 1841 the new manager was at pains to reassure the public that he had no connections with previous proprietor and that police constables would be present at every part of the house. In the end, the freeholder put the building up for auction but failed to attract a buyer. Finally, in 1849, it was demolished to build five houses.

Royal School of Needlework

Queen Victoria's third daughter, Princess Christian, founded a school for needlework in Sloane Street in 1872 to revive the art of embroidery. She was assisted by her friends in the Arts and Crafts movement, notably William Morris, his daughter May and Sir Edward Burne-Jones. One of the teachers was Margaret Macdonald, wife of the architect, Charles Rennie Mackintosh.

In 1892 the school was granted a site on the corner of Imperial Institute Road and Exhibition Road. When the handsome building, designed by Fairfax Wade, was leased to Imperial College, the school moved first to Princes Gate in 1949 and then in 1987 to Hampton Court. Their old building was demolished in 1962.

St Augustine's, Queen's Gate

St Augustine's began in 1865 when the Rev. Richard Chope, then curate of **Holy Trinity Brompton**, had an iron shed erected in his garden. A site was then found in an undeveloped part of Queen's Gate. From its earliest beginnings the church became a bastion of Anglo-Catholic worship.

The new church was built by William Butterfield in 1871 and set at an angle to the street. The building was in Butterfield's typical polychromatic style, with a brick exterior, and marble, coloured brick mosaics and glazed tile murals, a striking contrast with the white neo-classicism of Queen's Gate and the surrounding area.

A key feature of the interior is the eighteen decorative tile panels which tell the story of the bible from Adam and Eve to the ascension of Christ. In the 1920s all but the central two were covered in whitewash. With the support of John Betjeman, money was raised to remove the whitewash. In many places, however, the whitewash had sunk so deeply into the brickwork that it was impossible to remove, and so the bricks were painted to resemble Butterfield's original designs.

In the early 1980s, the Webber Douglas Academy of Dramatic Art moved into part of the church hall for use as rehearsal rooms.

133. *St Augustine's church, Queen's Gate, 1954.*

St Cuthbert's, Philbeach Gardens

Despite strong opposition and local jealousy, the curate at St Matthias, Henry Westall, was determined to build a church to serve the expanding population of West Kensington. The Bishop of London condemned the plans, declaring that there were not enough poor people in the area. Housed originally in an iron shed nicknamed by some as 'the dust bin', it developed into the grandest church in the area *(see ill. 51)*. The architect was Hugh Gough but owing to a lack of funds progress was piecemeal. The congregation were encouraged by Westall to contribute not only funds but time and skills to decorate the rather spartan interior. Led by skilled craftsmen their efforts produced a magnificent art deco interior. Westall was rewarded when he became the first incumbent, a position he was to hold until his death in 1924. Under his influence St Cuthbert's became the most flourishing High Church

foundation in Kensington. In 1958 the parish of St Matthias was amalgamated with St Cuthbert's, and St Matthias, at the corner of Warwick Road and Earl's Court Square, was demolished.

The church hall, completed in 1896, included a meeting hall, library, gymnasium and living accommodation for the curates. Today this is well used by community organisations such as St Mungo's and accommodates a very active drop-in centre for the homeless and vulnerable.

St John's Scarsdale Villas

St John's Presbyterian church in Scarsdale Villas was opened in May 1863. The building, by the Scottish architect J N McCulloch, was a disappointment to many owing to its plainness which was said gave it a "sense of depression".

St John's was badly damaged during an air raid in September 1940 and for a time the congregation joined its neighbours at Kensington Chapel until that too was hit. Although both congregations eventually moved back to their original buildings they were soon rejoined under the umbrella of the **United Reformed Church** based at the Kensington Chapel, Allen Street.

During its final years as an independent church St John's became known for staging the experimental religious drama, *The Man Born to be King* by Dorothy Sayers, which later enjoyed tremendous success on the radio. At this time depiction of Christ by an actor was highly controversial. The church was also the location for the earliest shows by the popular 1950s and

'60s entertainers Michael Flanders and Donald Swann.

But perhaps the greatest legacy was the appointment in 1952 of the young organist John Tavener. Many will remember his work for the funeral of **Diana, Princess of Wales** and he has done much to encourage the popularity of medieval liturgical singing. Tavener left St John's in 1973, his last festive occasion featuring a work for trumpet and organ. In 1975 St John's was sold to the Coptic Orthodox Church, St Mark's.

St Jude's, Courtfield Gardens

St Jude's church was one of the three churches designed by George and Henry **Godwin** and built on the **Gunter Estate**. The first was **St Mary's, The Boltons**, followed by St Jude's and St Luke's, Redcliffe Gardens. During this period of unprecedented speculative development, church building became very competitive. Usually a new church was seen as the culmination of a development but in the case of St Jude's, the church preceded the building of houses. Some members of the Anglican Low Church movement were dismayed by the spread of ritualistic services in the new parishes and determined to build their own church in Courtfield Gardens.

Funded in large part by the wealthy glove manufacturer John Derby Allcroft, St Jude's was built in 1870. It was described by William Pepperell, who conducted a survey of religious buildings in 1870s, as standing out "boldly, treeless and alone ... it has within three months collected one of the larg-

134. *St Jude's church. From The Builder, July 1870.*

est congregations to be met with around London". The original plain interior was embellished by Clayton and Bell stained glass windows, Minton and majolica tiling and alabaster and marble reredos and pulpit. Much of this was lost in September 1940 during a bombing raid but the interior has been restored to its original lightness.

St Mary Abbots

Although Kensington is mentioned in the Domesday Book, it was not until the 13th century that the **Abbot of Abingdon** established a church here as an independent parish. Little is known about this medieval building except that it had a 50-foot tower with a spire and clock, which was all that remained when the church was rebuilt in 1683. Sponsors for the new building included **William and Mary** and Princess Anne. It was described as "very large and spacious, built of brick and paved handsomely with Purbeck stone." Unfortunately the foundations were not so solid, and by 1704 the congregation was obliged to move to Holland House chapel while repairs were carried out. The whole church was replaced in 1772 with a red brick one.

For some 500 years St Mary Abbots was the only church serving the whole parish from Kensal to the boundary with Chelsea. As the population grew new parishes were established. **Holy Trinity, Brompton** was the first, quickly followed by St Barnabas, Addison Road; in all a total of 14 parishes were created over fifty years, mainly at the instigation of the Vicar of Kensington, Archdeacon John Sinclair.

The Bishop of London, Charles Blomfield thought that St Mary Abbots was the ugliest church in the diocese and it soon became the most dangerous as it was riddled with dry rot and the walls were bulging. Declared unsafe in 1866, Archdeacon Sinclair determined to build a new church that was "on a scale proportionate to the opulence and importance of a great Metropolitan parish."

The old building was demolished in 1869 and recorded in a series of photographs taken by Dr John **Merriman** from his house in Kensington Square. Sir George Gilbert Scott, who was working on the Albert Memorial at the time, was appointed architect. Many regard his building as a Gothic Revival masterpiece. Consecrated in 1872, the tower at 250 foot is said to be the tallest in London; this was

135. An 18th-century south-east view of St Mary Abbot's church, c.1750.

added in 1879 and houses ten bells, which still ring out. Visitors to the High Street on Thursday evenings can enjoy the weekly practice by the bell ringers.

On 14 March 1944 the church was hit by incendiary bombs which destroyed the roof, only a speedy response by the voluntary fire service prevented further damage. It is said that one of the firemen played hymns continuously on the church organ to prevent water entering the pipes. The new nave was designed by Romilly Craze and installed in 1955. With an active congregation, St Mary Abbots continues to be a popular and fashionable venue for weddings and other ceremonies. It is also an oasis of calm for those escaping from the busy High Street, with its regular lunchtime concerts, often performed by students from the Royal College of Music.

St Mary Abbots Hospital

In 1846 the Vestry purchased a site in Marloes Road from the Gunters to build a replacement for the small workhouse on Butts Field (now Kensington Gate). Thomas Allom designed a distinctive Jacobean style red-brick building with a clock turret. St Margaret and St John's parishes in Westminster also built a workhouse on the same site which incorporated some humane features such as married quarters for elderly inmates.

Both of the workhouses had small but primitive infirmaries. *The Lancet* in 1865 took up the cause predicting that if they were improved they could become "magnificent clinical hospitals instead of shreds and patches". When Westminster moved to St Stephen's on the Fulham Road, Kensington acquired the building for use as an

infirmary. By the turn of the century this was recognised as a general hospital with specialist departments. In 1929 it was taken over by the London County Council and renamed St Mary Abbots Hospital.

After the advent of the National Health Service in 1948, the hospital specialised in psychiatry, geriatrics and the chronic sick. In the 1980s with the building of the Chelsea and Westminster Hospital in Fulham Road, the hospital was sold and developed as a gated luxury housing complex called Kensington Green. Two remnants of the old workhouse survive, Allom's Stone Hall which is Grade I listed and the drinking fountain in the external wall with its text urging the poor to be free from "strong drink".

The hospital was the place where on 18 September 1970, rock guitarist Jimi Hendrix was taken following a drug overdose.

136. *Staff on parade at St Mary Abbot's Hospital in the 1930s.*

There he was certified as dead by a doctor who examined him in the back of the ambulance.

As a postscript it is worth noting that from 1978 to 1988 the hospital was home to the Anthony Nolan Trust. An old, disused laboratory was modernised and it was here that the Register of Bone Marrow Donors was set up. The closure was a wrench to the charity, as by 1988 there were over twenty scientists working there and some 100,000 donors had been tested. The Royal Free Hospital came to the rescue by providing alternative accommodation.

St Mary's, The Boltons

The church *(ill. 24)* was built in the late 1840s as the centre piece of Robert Gunter's new development, The Boltons. It was de-

signed by **George Godwin** the Younger and construction costs were met by the first vicar, Rev. Hogarth J. Swale. The tower and steeple were added in 1856 and cost £1000. Further alterations and embellishments were subsequently undertaken. Following extensive war damage, what remained of the Victorian interior was replaced in 1952 with a simpler whitewashed design. A notable member of the congregation was **Jenny Lind** Goldschmidt, a leading member of the church choir.

St Paul's, Onslow Gardens

Sir Charles Freake contributed most of the funds to build St Paul's as part of the Onslow Square development for **Smith's Charity**. The stone-built church, with its distinctive slender spire

in the Perpendicular style, opened in 1860. The last service was held on 1 May 1977 and since then the building has been used for administration purposes by **Holy Trinity, Brompton**.

There have been recent plans, to the designs of Norman Foster, to restore this Grade II listed building and provide a four-storey stone and glass extension, replacing the 1960s' vicarage and church hall. The building would house a Family Life Centre, a theological college for the Alpha Course, a vast auditorium seating 1000 and broadcasting facilities. Accommodation for the verger and curates would be built at the back. However, this scheme seems to have been abandoned.

137. St Paul's church, Onslow Gardens.

St Peter's, Cranley Gardens

The site for St Peter's Church was donated by **Smith's Charity** and erected by **Sir Charles Freake** in 1866-7. The large and prosperous congregation was mainly composed of retired army and civil service officers who helped fund several embellishments. The first organist from 1867 to 1871 was the composer **Sir Arthur Sullivan**. The last Anglican service was held in January 1973 when the parish was amalgamated with **St Mary's, The Boltons**. The building is now used by the Armenian Orthodox Church.

St Philip's, Earl's Court Road

St Philip's Church had its beginnings in 1842 when a room was taken on the corner of Warwick and Pembroke Gardens to serve as a chapel for the local poor. However, when the permanent site was selected it was much closer to the more affluent **Edwardes** and Pembroke Squares than to the alleys near the new railway. Half of the funds were supplied by the curate of St Barnabas, Joseph Claxton, who became the first vicar. The architect was his father-in-law Thomas Johnson, a well known Midlands church designer. The rest of the funds were raised by the congregation including ten shillings which was given in thanks for the discontinuance of the Sunday band in **Kensington Gardens**. The church was consecrated on 6 May 1857.

The next vicar, Walter Pennington, found it hard to exist on pew rents and when a new church in the locality was proposed he tried to obtain compensation for the effect this might have on his income. Decried by opponents as "a shameful sale of spiritualities" and "a disgrace to his sacred office", he was praised by his many friends for being kind hearted and generous and very good at obtaining theatre tickets for Drury Lane.

St Sarkis, Iverna Gardens

One of the smallest but prettiest churches in Kensington is St Sarkis, Iverna Gardens, built in the 1920s through the gift of the Armenian millionaire Calouste Gulbenkian.

After a series of massacres in their native land, Armenian immigrants began arriving in England, initially settling in Moss Side in Liverpool. As the community grew and spread to the capital after the First World War, their spiritual leader Dr

138. The Armenian St Sarkis church in Iverna Gardens, 1923.

Abel Abrahamian made an appeal for funds to build a church in London. Insufficient funds were raised, but the shipping magnate Gulbenkian came to the rescue. He agreed to provide £15,000 on condition that the church was dedicated to his parents, Mahtese Sarkis and Dirouhi Gulbenkian and designed in a traditional Armenian style.

The church is based on the little bell-tower of the St Haghpat Monastery. The interior is simple but this only serves to highlight the tiny chancel with its decoration of onyx, marble, alabaster and lapis lazuli with relief gilding designed by the Bromsgrove Guild.

The Turkish invasion of Cyprus in 1974 encouraged many Armenians to leave the island and settle in England. St Sarkis was unable to cope with this influx and extra accommodation was taken at the redundant **St Peter's Church** in Cranley Gardens.

St Stephen's, Southwell Gardens

St Stephen's church is probably best known for its association with **T S Eliot**, who served as a churchwarden here for many years.

Archdeacon John Sinclair built a small iron mission opposite what is now Gloucester Road station to cater for a growing population. In 1867 a stone building, designed by Joseph Peacock, more suitable for a large and fashionable congregation, was built.

In its early days the liturgy was low Anglican but over the years it moved towards Anglo-Catholicism. In 1890 the vicar, the Rev. Lord Victor Seymour, considering the décor 'unseemly', commissioned G F Bodley to recommend and carry out changes. These included a new altar piece and a chapel dedicated to the Virgin Mary.

In 1996 St Stephen's was in the news when its vicar, verger and thirty-four members of its congregation, left to join the Roman Catholic Church over the issue of women priests in the Church of England.

Scarsdale House

Scarsdale House stood at the top of Wright's Lane until it was swallowed up by **Pontings** in the 1920s. Today, Boots the chemist and modern office blocks stand on the site.

Built by a City mercer, Francis Barry, in 1690 it stood behind high walls in four acres of garden that included a canal and a fishpond. By 1753 it had been purchased by a stable keeper and coachbuilder, Gregory Wright.

In its early years residents included the Duchess of Monmouth, widow of the rebel Duke and the wool merchant and one time Lord Mayor of London, Sir Humphrey Edwin. The Curzon family took the freehold in 1720 and it was from one of their titles that the mansion got its name. Inevitably it was soon in use as a school and part of the grounds sold off.

Fortuitously, Edward Cecil Curzon, a wealthy antiquarian, came to the rescue enlarging and refurbishing the house. It was at this time that the radical **William Cobbett** set off on his 'Rural Rides' from a cottage just behind Scarsdale House.

However the encroachment of the railway continued and in the 1890s Pontings took over, creating a 'tea and retiring room for ladies' in the remnants of the old house.

The Science Museum

The Science Museum's renowned collections grew out of the Science & Art Department which established the South Kensington Museum in 1857. The collections were greatly enriched when the Patent Museum passed on its stock of patent models to the science collections, including priceless objects such as Stephenson's 'Rocket' and Arkwright's original textile machinery. Professor T H Huxley pleaded for a separate museum for science so that the collection could be "removed from its present filthy, repulsive, unwholesome sheds". His wish was granted in 1909 when the Science Museum and the **Victoria & Albert Museum** were formally separated.

Unfortunately, building was delayed – work began in 1914 but the first block was only formally opened by King George V in 1928 and not completed until 1961. Today it is one of the world's outstanding museums celebrating man's greatest inventions and achievements.

When a Board of Trustees took over in 1983 a period of rapid development followed. Much to the delight of children new interactive galleries, such as Launch Pad and Flight Lab were opened and a busy programme of activities including night sleepovers and birthday parties was offered. New galleries, including the Secret Life of the Home, and facilities such as the IMAX 3D cinema have recently been introduced.

Jean Sibelius

Sibelius (1865-1957) was born in Hameenlina, Finland to a Swedish speaking family but his parents chose to have him educated in Finnish. A fierce nationalist, much of his work shows his strong love of his country and its culture. Starting life as a lawyer he quit this to study music, producing a series of symphonies from 1892 based on the Finnish epic *Kalevala*. After this early success the government gave him a grant, allowing him to concentrate fully on his music. He went on to become Finland's greatest composer, producing symphonic poems, like the nationalistic *Finlandia* of 1899, seven symphonies and a violin concerto amongst other works. Then, in 1925, he destroyed the score for an eighth symphony and spent the last thirty years of his life refusing to write another song or speak

139. Jean Sibelius.

about his existing work.

He spent a year in Kensington, living at 15 Gloucester Walk in 1909.

140. The slums of Market Court, c.1865.

Slums

Kensington's population figures tell their own story. At the beginning of the 19th century, 8,600 people lived in the Borough; this increased to 163,000 in 1889. Kensington became immensely overcrowded, with much closely-packed slum housing and poor sanitation. Disease was rife. Even though Kensington was prosperous, conditions were poor in the secret slums just off Kensington High Street including Market Court, Gardener's Buildings and Brown's Buildings. The most notorious was Jennings' Buildings, described in the local paper as "Truly horrible to conceive ... in that narrow space are crammed nearly 1500 living souls". Mainly Irish labourers, they worked in the market gardens and later on building sites.

These rookeries were cleared away by 1867 with many of the displaced inhabitants moving to Notting Dale.

Smith's Charity

The income for this charity, founded by the will of Alderman Henry Smith, a prominent salter who died in 1627, came from the purchase of some 70 acres in Brompton. The irregular shaped plot stretched from north of the Fulham Road to south of Old Brompton Road and from Yeoman's Row to Evelyn Gardens. It was set up to pay ransom for English sailors captured and enslaved by Barbary pirates, and Henry Smith's poor relations. The Trustees, as the supply of captives and poor kindred dwindled and profits increased, widened the aims of the charity, primarily into medical fields. The Board of Trustees was established in 1658 and recruited from the ranks of the aristocracy and landed gentry. Membership was often passed from father to son.

Michael Novosielski was the first developer of its land, taking leases on 14 acres in Brompton Road; unfortunately none of his buildings survive. Large parts of the estate continued to be leased by profitable horticultural nurseries including Harrison, Thomas Gibb and William Malcolm.

In 1929 George Basevi was appointed architect and with the builders James Bonin and his sons began to transform the area. Their architectural legacy remains and Pelham Crescent and Egerton Crescent are rightly seen as amongst the best late Georgian developments in Kensington. All the streets on the estate were named after the Trustees thus making it easy to identify their properties today.

On the Fulham Road, in 1844, the Hospital for Consumption and Diseases of the Chest, better known as Brompton Hospital, was erected to Basevi's designs. The freehold was transferred to the Hospital's Trustees a few

141 and 142. Two developments on the Smith's Charity estate. Above is Pelham Crescent and below Evelyn Gardens, both photographed c.1905.

Brompton Hospital, as Basevi's building was known, has now been converted into luxury flats.

In 1845 Basevi fell to his death while working on Ely Cathedral and two years later the Bonins went bankrupt. This heralded the entrance of **Sir Charles Freake**, who worked on the estate from 1845 to 1884, and Cluttons, who took over as Surveyors. Together they built some 330 large houses, one hundred coach houses and stables and two churches. The major developments were Onslow Square and Gardens, Cranley Gardens and Place, Sydney Place, **Cromwell Road** and Evelyn Gardens. In 1995 the estate, valued at £282 million and producing an annual income of £11 million, was sold to the Wellcome Trust.

C P Snow

The phrase 'Corridors of Power' frequently appears in the press but its origin was the title of a book by Charles Percy Snow (1905-1980) published in 1964, the year he moved into 199 Cromwell Road. That same year he was created a Labour life peer, Baron Snow of Leicester.

Lewis Eliot is the narrator of C P Snow's best-known series of works, *Strangers and Brothers*, and there are many parallels with Snow's own life and career. Both were born in provincial towns, went on to be Fellows at Cambridge and took up Government posts. Snow was appointed by Harold Wilson as Parliamentary Secretary at the Ministry of Technology from 1964 to 1966.

Another contribution by Snow to the lexicon was 'Two Cultures'. He gave a series of lec-

143. C P Snow.

tures discussing the breakdown in communication between science and the humanities which he felt was very damaging. In 1975, the year he left Cromwell Road for Eaton Terrace, his biography of Anthony Trollope appeared.

He was married to the novelist Pamela Hansford Johnson.

Spies

Few will be surprised given the large number of embassies, in particular the Soviet Embassy in **Kensington Palace Gardens**, that spies operated in the area. Many references can be found in biographies to dead letter drops and meetings in Kensington at such places as the **Odeon** cinema, **Brompton Oratory** and the statue of Assisi outside Holy Trinity. Indeed the area was a hive of espionage activity during the Cold War. But there were earlier precedents.

A recent TV drama the *Reilly Ace of Spies* told the story of the most successful spy employed by the British Secret Service, Sidney Reilly. Born Sigmund Georgievich Rosenblum in Russia in 1874 he attended the

144. 6 & 7 Kensington Palace Gardens where the 'London Cage' was based during the Second World War.

Royal School of Mines, South Kensington in 1905. A brilliant scholar and linguist he then went on to Trinity College, Cambridge giving 63 Earl's Court Square as his address. Before the First World War he was sent to Germany and with the outbreak of hostilities to Russia. In 1924 with Arthur Gregory he was involved with forging the Zinoviev Letter and its publication in the *Daily Mail*. The forged letter urged British Communists to promote revolution through seditious acts and contributed to the fall of Ramsey MacDonald's Labour Government in 1924. In 1925 Reilly was sent back to Russia but his luck ran out and he was captured and shot.

William Joyce, better known as Lord Haw Haw, was living at 38 Onslow Gardens in 1938. In August 1939 he left for Germany where he made his infamous broadcasts.

Numbers 6-7 **Kensington Palace Gardens** contained an army interrogation centre soon after the Dunkirk evacuation in 1940. Known as the Cage, it was run by Colonel Alexander. Recent revelations led to condemnation of some of the interrogation techniques. Over 3,500 men passed through the Cage and its five cells.

Following on from their expertise in interrogating POWs in 1944 the unit took over investigation of war criminals prior to their trials. This included those involved in the murders of fifty RAF officers after their escape from Stalag Luft III in 1944, so memorably retold in *The Great Escape*. It is also believed that Rudolf Hess was held here. In 1948 the building was taken by the Russian Federation for their Chancery Section.

As the Russians steadily built up their presence in Kensington Palace Gardens so did the rumours of espionage and counter espionage increase. Peter Wright in his controversial book *Spycatcher* confirmed some of the stories. Certainly it was the base for KGB operators including Oleg Gordievsky, head of the London group, who later turned out to be a double agent. John Vassall, recruited in Moscow via a 'honey trap', was arrested in 1962 and released ten years, later made several references to Kensington connections. These were contained in documents released by The National Archives in June 2006. In 1972 Maureen Bingham, wife of a naval officer, walked into the Embassy and offered her husband's services as a spy. She was paid £2,800 for her husband's notebooks but their career was short lived when after a terrifying encounter with his KGB handlers David Bingham confessed to the police.

But perhaps the most famous name is Kim Philby, a double agent who worked for the KGB for more than thirty years before discovery but was also recruited by MI6. During the 1950s he lived with his family in Grove Court, Holly Mews just off the Fulham Road behind Evelyn Gardens. For a while under suspicion, the Grove Court press conference he gave was one of his greatest bluffs and within six months he was working again for MI6. He escaped to Moscow in 1963 but his mother continued to live in the flat.

Spying was by no means restricted to the Russians, as in 1954 the Board of Admiralty took over the South Kensington Hotel, 35-45 Queen's Gate Terrace for use as quarters for Wrens and the Joint Services School of Languages, a euphemism for MI6. The property was given up in 1992 and is now called Furze House.

Close to Holland Park the Russians, Americans and British all set up spy posts. The first to arrive were the Russians who purchased nos. 9, 10, 11 Earl's Terrace, which had been bombed during the war, as accommodation for 'Embassy staff'. When the houses were recently renovated a padded cell was discovered. The CIA had a surveillance base in **Edwardes Square** as did M15 in Leonard Court on the High Street. What goes on today behind closed doors is a matter for conjecture.

Sir Leslie Stephen

A blue plaque on 22 Hyde Park Gate commemorates the residency of Sir Leslie Stephen (1832-1904), first editor of *The Dictionary of National Biography* and two of his children, Vanessa Bell and Virginia Woolf, who were born and raised there.

Sir Leslie came from a prominent family. His father was Sir John Stephen, under-secretary to the Colonial Office, and his brother was a High Court judge. A sickly child, he changed at Cambridge, becoming both a committed academic and a great sportsman. He married Harriet 'Minnie' Thackeray in 1867 moving in with her and her sister Anne to 16 Onslow Gardens. They later lived with their daughter Laura at Southwell Gardens before leaving London.

Returning to London after Harriet's death in 1875, he moved into "a little backwater of a street" called Hyde Park Gate. Here he married a neighbour, Julia Duckworth, a niece of the pioneer photographer Julia Margaret Cameron. They had four children and lived a generally happy life spoilt by occasional melancholy, as recorded in Woolf's *Moment of Being*. He died at home in 1904.

Vanessa was born there in 1879. She was a painter, decorative designer and leading member of the Bloomsbury Group. Largely educated at home she took drawing lessons from Ebenezer Cook before she attended Sir Arthur Cope's art school in 1896. She then studied painting at the Royal Academy Schools in 1899.

She took on the role of housekeeper after her mother's death in 1895, a difficult task in such a demanding family, especially as she was trying to develop her artistic skills at the same time.

Virginia was born in 1882 and called 'the Goat' by her siblings. When she was nine she started a weekly paper, *The Hyde Park Gate News*, chronicling family doings in their Kensington and Cornwall homes. It was circulated to friends and neighbours. She was thirteen when her mother died, and it was the

145. *Sir Leslie Stephen; oil painting by G F Watts.*

first time that she suffered symptoms of her depression which was to plague her life. Many references can be found in her novels to people and places associated with Kensington.

Following Sir Leslie's death, the Stephen sisters, together with their brothers Adrian and Thoby, moved to Gordon Square in Bloomsbury in 1906. Here they would meet writers, artists and intellectuals who would come to be known as the Bloomsbury group.

Street names

Much can be learnt about an area's history from the origins of its street names. They can provide useful clues about what used to be on the site, who developed or built upon it, and what famous people had associations. Prior to the mid-nineteenth century developers were free to select names at whim but with the rapid development of London more control was required. This role was first performed by the Metropolitan Board of Works and then by its successors the LCC and GLC. When the latter body was dissolved this function was transferred to the boroughs. However the names adopted were, and still are, usually based on an area's history or associations. In the descriptions below the date given in brackets is the year of official naming, not always the same as construction.

Given the Borough's Royal connections it is not surprising that many names, especially around **Kensington Palace**, reflect this. Most are obvious such as Queen's Gate, Victoria Road, and Prince of Wales Terrace. Others are less so, such as **Cornwall Gardens** (1864), named in honour of Prince Albert, Duke of Cornwall's coming of age in the year the gardens were laid out in 1862.

Around **St Mary Abbot's Church** and just off the High Street names recalling feudal ownership and places can be found. The De Veres were Lords of the Manor for 500 years, hence De Vere Gardens (1875); they gave a portion to the **Abbots of Abingdon** leading to the numerous Abingdons and Abbots in local street names. Cope Place (1911) is named after Sir Walter Cope who built Holland House and was Lord of the Manor. Warwick Road (1847) is named for the Earls of Warwick and Holland, Lords of the Manor of Earl's Court in the 17th and 18th centuries. Earl's Court Road (1846) has the same origins and marks the location of their court house, demolished in 1867 to build Earl's Court Station. Cheniston Gardens (1880) recalls the Anglo-Saxon derivation of Kensington. Courtfield Gardens (1873) derives from a former field name, Courtefeld,

146. *Gilston Road, on the Gunter Estate, c.1905, named after a family property.*

used in 1642 as does Redfield Lane (1885). Kenway Road (1873) is on the line of a footpath on the 'way to Kensington'.

Brompton was known for its villas and **nurseries** giving rise to a rich crop of names. Selwood Terrace (1826) was built on Richard Selwood's Nursery and William Stratford owned four acres of market garden bordering Stratford Road.

Streets named after villas along the Old Brompton Road include Rosary Gardens (1881), Clareville Grove (1875), Coleherne Road (1876), Hereford Square and Creswell Gardens (1885) after Creswell Lodge, noted for an extensive aviary and conservatory. Two houses of note are remembered in Kensington, Eldon Lodge (Eldon Road 1852), home to animal painter Alfred Hitchen Corbould and **Scarsdale House** (Scarsdale Villas 1856) at the top of Wright's Lane was formerly owned by the Curzon family,

created Barons Scarsdale in 1761. Wright's Lane (1795) is named after its builder Gregory Wright.

Commemorating events is another popular choice, for example Inkerman (1855) and Alma (1862) Terraces, after battles during the Crimea War.

Worthy local notables are also remembered. Lecky Street (1937) is named for the historian **William Lecky** who lived nearby at 38 Onslow Gardens. William Pater (1839-1894) the author and critic who lived at 12 Earl's Terrace is recalled in Pater Street (1905). Derry Street (1938) is named after the Derry family, one of the founders of **Derry & Toms,** and Foulis Terrace (1856) for Sir Henry Foulis who founded **Brompton Hospital** chapel in 1849. Statesmen remembered include the Duke of Wellington in Douro Place (1846) – one of his titles was Baron Douro, and **George Canning** who lived at Orford Lodge

(later Gloucester Lodge) near Canning Place (1847). Maria, Duchess of Gloucester, lived at Gloucester Lodge till her death in 1807. The Lodge was sited opposite what is today Gloucester Road station.

Trying to work out the complex estate ownership in southern Kensington is made much easier by looking at street names. Each of the landowners followed a set pattern when selecting names. The Trustees of **Smith's Charity** used their own names. They included the Earl of Onslow (Viscount Cranley is the title taken by the eldest son); the Hon. Francis Egerton; John Robert, Viscount Sydney; William Sumner and Henry Thomas Pelham, Earl of Chichester. Looking at a map of the area it is now easy to see the boundary of their estate. The Earls of **Harrington** also used family names hence Stanhope Gardens (1868) and Petersham Lane (1923). Elvaston Mews

(1866) comes from Elvaston Castle, Derbyshire one of their country seats. The same applies to the **Alexander Estate** where the owner John Thurloe is remembered in Thurloe Square (1827). Astwood Mews (1873) derives from a place in Buckinghamshire where he once lived.

The two largest land owners, the Edwardes and the Gunters, adopted place names from their counties, Pembrokeshire and Yorkshire respectively. On the **Edwardes Estate** examples include Longridge Road (1872), Marloes Road (1872), Nevern Square (1872), Trebovir Road (1911), Philbeach Gardens (1875) and Templeton Place (1886) all in Pembrokeshire. The **Gunters** were a little more adventurous. Barkston Ash and Knaresborough were both parliamentary seats held by Sir Robert Gunter. Gledhow Gardens (1869) comes from Gledhow Hall home of Jane Benyan, Sir Robert's wife; Gilston and Tregunter are also family houses, this time in Brecknockshire. Yorkshire villages names used include Bramham, Collingham, Laverton, Netherton, all of which are in the neighbourhood of Sir Robert's family seat Wetherby Grange.

Suffrage shops

For those outside the 'Votes for Women' movement, suffrage shops provided a friendlier environment than a formal office, but at the same time gave the movement a high-street presence. The Shops provided prominent advertising space and were accessible recruiting places. Many drew in a public that would not ordinarily have ventured into a campaign office.

'Nobody said so in committee, but I do not believe that a single member of that serious and grown-up group of the Kensington Suffragettes was above feeling a secret thrill of glee at the thought of keeping shop at last' wrote Evelyn Sharp on the opening of Kensington's store.

The trend for opening shops grew, with 1909 seeing the emergence of more in such places as Edinburgh, Bristol and Bradford. In 1913, the Kensington branch, which had been one of the first to open, reported annual sales of the Women's Social & Political Union's (WSPU) newspaper of almost 18,000 – nearly 70 copies for each working day.

Suffrage shops came to be 'feminine' spaces, with an emphasis on notions of middle-class domesticity and personal adornment. In some cases the 'Votes for Women' issues were at risk of being subsumed beneath attempts to market merchandise in a pleasing format. The Kensington shop appealed to "domestic friends to remember us when making jam and to give a pot or two tied up with ribbons for our window. Gifts of flowers are greatly welcomed for the same purpose" – not usually concerns commonly associated with a militant campaign.

There were major window-smashing campaigns of Suffrage Shops, which saw destruction of premises in Oxford Street, Regent Street and Piccadilly. But not all attacks were as violent: the Kensington branch described "the ubiquitous small boy...the natural enemy of all change and all progress ... when there is snow on the ground he has an easy weapon to hand".

Within the papers of Sylvia Pankhurst, can be found the Kensington shop's accounts – 1913 for instance saw the store's receipts total £214 10s, 8d, and items such as tea, soap and cigarettes "added satisfactorily to the yearly income."

Suffragettes

In 1865 a group of women from the **Kensington Society** organised a petition that demanded that women should have the same political rights as men. Following the defeat of their amendment, added by John Stuart Mill to the Reform Act, they decided to form the London Society for Women's Suffrage. Similar societies were formed and eventually seventeen of these groups joined together to form the National Union of Women's Suffrage Societies.

In 1903 the Women's Social and Political Union (WSPU) was founded by Emmeline Pankhurst and her daughters Christabel and Sylvia. They wanted women to have the right to vote and they were not prepared to wait. The Union became better known as the Suffragettes. They decided to use violence to get what they wanted. Their patience was exasperated when in 1905, MP's 'talked out' moves to give women the vote. In a meeting held after this setback, a call for a more militant action was proposed, even if this meant breaking the law. It wasn't long before their motto 'Deeds not words' came into effect.

A handbill advertising a protest meeting in Parliament Square was issued by Mrs. Pankhurst, who also wrote to the Prime Minister, demanding a statement on women's right to vote. When this was rebuffed, 'The Mænads' as *The Times* called them, turned to more violent methods. One group attacked stores in Knightsbridge, Brompton Road and Kensington High Street. The outbreak was unexpected and few constables were about. Sentences for the window smashers ranged from seven days to two months, but those causing damage over £5 were more severely dealt with; sentences ranged from four to eight months.

Women over the age of thirty were finally given the right to vote in 1918, and extended to women over 21 in 1928.

Sir Arthur Sullivan

Arthur Seymour Sullivan (1842-1900) was born in Lambeth, son of a military bandmaster. By the age of 8, he was proficient with all the instruments in the band. Following a stay at private school in Bayswater, he was admitted to the choir of the Chapel Royal, attending its school in Cheyne Walk. While there, he began to compose anthems and songs. In 1856, he received the first Mendelssohn prize and became a student at the Royal Academy of Music until 1858. He then continued his studies at Leipzig, where he also took up conducting. He held the post of organist at St Peter's, from the day of its consecration until 1872, and was appointed the first Principal of the National Training School for Music in 1876.

Sir Arthur was knighted for his contribution to serious music but it is for his operatic collaboration with the librettist **W S Gilbert** that he is best known. Richard D'Oyly Carte, owner of the Savoy Theatre,

147. *Sir Arthur Sullivan, from the painting by Sir John Millais.*

brought the two together in 1875 and their first production, *Trial by Jury*, was followed by 13 more culminating in *The Grand Duke* in 1896. The 1999 film *Topsy-Turvey* gave an insight into their somewhat strained relationship, especially in the later years.

Kay Summersby

In wartime gossip spread like wildfire and one story certainly did the rounds in Kensington, the close friendship between General Dwight Eisenhower (Ike) and his attractive driver-cum-secretary Kay Summersby (1908-1975).

Kay was a driver with the Auxiliary Fire Service and based at the 8-X station headquarters in Elvaston Mews, living in a flat just round the corner. Before the war the Anglo-Irish Kay had worked as a model for the House of Worth and was described as

148. General Dwight Eisenhower.

a great beauty. When Eisenhower was posted to London in 1942 as Commander of US forces in London she became his driver, a position she held throughout the war.

In her first book *Ike was my Boss* written in 1948, Kay gave a history of her work for him, but glossed over their alleged relationship. Her second book *Past Forgetting; My Love Affair with Dwight D Eisenhower*, written after she was diagnosed with cancer and published after her death, was a different matter. The truth will never be known. Eisenhower's friends denied the story saying it was pure fantasy on her part, but there is no doubt that they were close. His recently discovered diaries from those years were found to be mainly written by Kay. Mamie, his wife, was jealous of Kay's closeness to her husband. Lee Remick played Kay in two films on Ike's wartime years.

Augustus Frederick, Duke of Sussex

The Duke of Sussex (1773-1843), George III's sixth son, lived in apartments in Kensington Palace. He became a staunch supporter of Caroline of Brunswick, the estranged wife of his brother the Prince Regent, and his neighbour at the Palace. The Duke, while being amiable, intelligent and progressive was also excessively vain. He was particularly proud of his voice which he claimed spanned three octaves, and he was rather eccentric. Against the Royal Marriage Act he secretly married Lady Augusta Murray with whom he had two children, an act that led to him being disinherited. He also married Celia Underwood twice!

Another Royal asthmatic with poor eyesight, he built up a magnificent library and collection of clocks and watches which left him in serious debt. He was also an active freemason and became a Grand Master. The young **Victoria** was said to be frightened by her uncle, fear that was overcome as he gave her away at her wedding to Prince Albert. Shortly before William IV's death the brothers were reconciled. At his own request the Duke of Sussex was buried in the newly opened Kensal Green Cemetery.

Tattersall's

Once Tattersall's, the world famous bloodstock auctioneers, had a significant presence in the area both professionally and personally, it is now only commemorated locally as a name for a public house.

Richard Tattersall, the firm's founder, was a stud groom to the second Duke of Kingston who resided at no 3 Knightsbridge and described by the waspish Horace Walpole as a "very weak man, of the greatest beauty and finest person in England". Richard on the other hand was cut from a different cloth and widely regarded as a man of integrity. Following his employer's death, he set himself up as an auctioneer in 1766. He established premises near Hyde Park Corner with stables, loose boxes and an enclosure for trying out horses. There were

149. Tattersall's auction rooms at Knightsbridge Green in 1869.

150. *Tattersall's old auction rooms near the site of St George's Hospital at Hyde Park Corner. Aquatint by Pugin and Rowlandson, 1809.*

also subscription rooms for members of the Jockey Club, which became both the social centre for members of the racing fraternity and in time the regulatory body for betting on the turf. By 1782 the Tattersall name was already used in a stage play, a clear indication of success.

With the expiry of the lease in 1865 the premises were demolished to make way for an extension to St George's hospital. A two-acre site was found in Knightsbridge Green, on the site of the now-doomed Bowater House. Illustrations show the two major features, the grand entrance arch and the auction ring. This was housed in a vast hall covered by a glass roof and surrounded by galleries which

cost £30,000. In 1909 London historian E. Beresford Chancellor wrote "one could no more imagine the town without it than one could conceive it without St Paul's or Charing Cross Station". Alas the unimaginable happened and in 1939 Tattersall's moved out to Newmarket but the famous entrance arch was moved to the course and now stands proudly in the car park.

Edmund Tattersall, head of the firm in the mid-nineteenth century, with his family were the last residents of Coleherne House before it was demolished to make way for **Coleherne Court**. They lived here from 1865 to 1898.

Ellen Terry

Ellen Terry (1847-1928), married three times, was also involved in numerous relationships during her lifetime. After a brief and disastrous first marriage to the painter, George Frederick Watts in 1864, Terry established herself as Britain's leading Shakespearean actress. In 1876 she married Charles Kelly but by 1878 had formed both a personal and professional partnership with Sir Henry Irving, actor-manager of the Lyceum. Working closely with Irving she dominated English theatre for over twenty years. She lived at 33 Longridge Road from 1878 to 1889 and from 1889 to 1902 at 22 Barkston Gardens. These were the years of her greatest

151. Ellen Terry.

William Makepeace Thackeray

Thackeray (1811-1863) was born in Calcutta, India to Richmond Thackeray and Anne Becher. After dropping out of Cambridge he spent his early days flitting between Britain, France and Germany. After marrying Anne Isabella in Paris in 1836 he finally settled in London. They had three daughters: Anne, Jane and Harriet. His wife later became mentally ill following the birth of her youngest child, causing serious problems between Thackeray and his mother-in-law, who blamed him for her daughter's condition.

After many false starts his career took off as a journalist. Between 1840 and 1847 he wrote 386 pieces and three books under numerous pseudonyms for several magazines. Then, in 1847, *Punch* printed his masterpiece *Vanity Fair* in serial form. This made him £1200, a household name and ensured his future

152. William Thackeray, from the painting by Samuel Laurence.

fame. Her departure from Barkston Gardens coincided with the ending of her partnership with Irving. She then took on a new career as a theatrical manager.

Her third marriage in 1907 to American actor James Carew, nearly thirty years her junior, foundered after two years. As her close friend George Bernard Shaw was to note wryly, "one might say that her marriages were adventures and her friendships enduring". Her grandnephew, **Sir John Gielgud**, also became an acclaimed actor. She became a Dame Grand Cross of the British Empire (GBE) in 1925.

153. Thackeray's house in Young Street.

154. Ernest Thesiger.

works would be best sellers. He was also editor of the hugely successful *Cornhill Magazine* from 1860.

Following his journalistic successes in 1846 he bought a house at 16 Young Street, his 'feudal castle', where his adored daughters were at last able to join him. Here he wrote *Vanity Fair*, *Pendennis* and *Henry Esmond*, and hosted parties for the celebrities of the day. Then in 1853 he moved to the more fashionable Onslow Square to please his daughters before settling at 2 Palace Green in 1860 to enjoy his golden years. He died there on Christmas Eve in 1863.

Ernest Thesiger

Ernest Thesiger (1879-1961), who specialised in playing snooty upper crust Englishmen, was the grandson of a Lord Chancellor. Eschewing the Civil Service in favour of the Slade School of Fine Art, he became a member of a homosexual circle which included Willie Ranken and Oscar Wilde's friend Robert Ross, through whom he became an understudy at the St James's Theatre. Wounded in the Great War, Thesiger in 1917 married Janette, Willie Ranken's sister, moving into 6 Montpelier Terrace. The marriage was never consummated but was conven-

ient for both parties, Janette being in love with the poet Margaret Jourdain. Ernest, outwardly conformist, delighted in shocking dinner party guests by revealing green painted toenails and pearls worn next to his skin. He returned successfully to the stage, winning Shaw's approval as a perfect Professor Higgins and as the first Dauphin in *Saint Joan*. He also appeared in drag in the 1925 *Cochran Revue* and played Gaveston, the King's favourite in *Edward II*. In 1927 Thesiger published his autobiography, entitled *Practically True*. Allegedly he charged £50 for a mention in it – and £75 for an omission. Thesiger lived at 8 St George's Court, Gloucester Road, from 1939 until his death.

Sir Benjamin Thompson (Count Rumford)

The renowned physicist and inventor, Benjamin Thompson (1753-1814), was born in Woburn, Massachusetts. Despite good results at school he was not a successful apprentice or student at Harvard. This was due to his fascination with invention, which allegedly resulted in a large explosion at a shop where he was working. He married Sarah Walker in 1772 and they had a daughter. After her death he married Marie Paulze in 1805 but they separated in 1809.

Working as a teacher and landowner in Rumford, Massachusetts he was later made a major in the local regiment. Forced to flee to Boston, abandoning his family, he then embarked on a convoluted career as a Royalist, fighting for Britain. He left for England in 1783, joined the Royal Society, and then headed on to Bavaria. Joining the Bavarian war department in 1784, he conducted experiments into clothing, nutrition and heat and was made Count Rumford in 1792. His inventions include warmer clothing, a stove, the Rumford lamp and a new theory of heat convection.

Returning to London in 1799 Thompson founded the Royal Institution on Albermarle Street, where he lived until moving to 168 Brompton Road. During this time Thompson was much parodied for his self-importance and aggressive nature, but was also admired for his scientific brilliance and the introduction of new science and inventions to the public through his Institution. He moved to Paris in 1802.

Sir Herbert Beerbohm Tree

Born in Pembridge Villas as Herbert Draper Beerbohm (1853-1917), he took the stage name Tree in the 1870s. His younger half-brother was the parodist

155. Sir Herbert Beerbohm Tree.

and caricaturist Max Beerbohm and together they spent their childhood at 57 Palace Gardens Terrace. He attended schools across England and one in Germany.

After leaving school he became a clerk in the family business. Success on the amateur circuit led to his first professional appearance as Grimaldi in *The Life of an Actress* at the Globe Theatre in 1878. Although an excellent and popular actor he still struggled with his lines. One contemporary remembers that he "with fertile invention posted prompters under tables, behind rocks, jutting walls or ancient oaks as he moved in well-disguised anguish from cache to cache."

In 1883 he married actress Maud Holt with whom he had three daughters. Between 1891 and 1901 they lived at 31 Rosary Gardens. Tree fathered several illegitimate children, including film director Carol Reed and Peter Reed, the father of actor Oliver Reed. He was knighted in 1909.

Taking the lease of the Haymarket Theatre in 1887 he became an actor-manager. He produced an unusual mix of Shakespeare, early farces and contemporary social plays, including the first staging of Wilde's *A Woman of No Importance* and *The Importance of Being Earnest*. In 1897 he built Her Majesty's Theatre and staged the English premiere of Shaw's *Pygmalion* in 1914, playing Professor Higgins to Mrs Patrick Campbell's Eliza. When Shaw complained about the addition of a happy ending, Tree replied, "My ending makes money, you ought to be grateful."

His greatest legacy was the founding of the Royal Academy of Dramatic Art (RADA) in 1904, which remains the world's foremost drama school.

The Troubadour, Old Brompton Road

The humble coffee house became a cultural hothouse in the 1950s. Centres for rebellion and a bohemian way-of-life, they thrived, especially in Earl's Court. The most famous of these was the Troubadour, founded by Michael and Sheila Von Bloemen in 1954. Throughout the 1950s and '60s The Troubadour was one of the centres of intellectual and artistic life. This is where *Private Eye* was first distributed and where the early Ban the Bomb meetings were held, and also where the Black Panthers met when they left Paris. Bob Dylan first performed here and Paul Simon, Sammy Davis Jnr and Jimi Hendrix all played here, as well as myriads of other stars of the time. Poetry readings were a particular favourite with locals.

The Von Boemens sold the Troubadour to Bruce Rogerson

Tucker's Candle Factory

People complaining of pollution on the High Street today would have been appalled by the noxious fumes and thick black smoke emanating from Tucker's Candle factory. This, located just behind the High Street where the Derry & Toms building stands, started production in the mid eighteenth century and only ceased in 1908.

James Wheble, who lived at 36 Kensington Square, founded the factory in 1766. A well known Catholic he was succeeded by John Kendall, one of the founders of the area's first Catholic chapel in Holland Street. When he died the business was bought by Francis Tucker, a candle maker from South Molton Street. The office and shop were on the High Street but the sprawling works filled the space between the railway lines and Burden Mews.

Unsurprisingly, the firm was one of the foremost suppliers of

There's always something going on at

The Troubadour

265, OLD BROMPTON ROAD, LONDON, S.W.5.

LONDON'S OLDEST FOLK CLUB

NOVEMBER PROGRAMME

Tuesdays at 9.30 p.m.

7th	JOHNIE WINCH... DENNIS & VANESSA
14th	CLEM FLOYD
21st	TREVOR CROZIER
28th	COME ALL YE

Saturdays at 10.30 p.m.

4th	SPECIAL ATTRACTION (SEE BACK)
11th	THE LEESIDERS
18th	COLIN WILKIE & SHIRLEY HART
25th	AL STEWART

Sundays at 9.30 p.m.

5th	THE FO'C'SLE
12th	ALASDAIR CLAYRE & TOM BROWNE
19th	STEFAN ZOBEL
26th	THE PUNCHBOWL THREE

156. A Troubadour programme of 1969.

in 1970 who made sure the spirit of the place remained unchanged, and he sold it to the current owners, Simon and Susie Thornhill. The venture was such a success that the Thornhills acquired the adjoining two shops, totally refurbishing them. By the end of 2002, The Troubadour had more than doubled in size, offering extras such as a delicatessen and a much enhanced café. In July 2002 the refurbished Club reopened but thankfully the spirit still continues.

157. The smoking chimneys of Tucker's Candle factory on Kensington High Street in 1858. The site is now covered by the railway and the Derry & Toms building.

candles to Roman Catholic churches all over the country. In 1900 a new factory was opened in Putney which led to a decline in the Kensington business. The company went into liquidation in 1908 and the name and stock were taken up by Price's Patent Candle Company. Production was continued at Putney, Cricklewood and Battersea. The Kensington site was sold to Derry & Toms and the Crown.

The Underground

The advent of Underground railways from 1865 was to have a dramatic impact on the development of southern Kensington. Such residential areas were very attractive to railway companies and in this case cheaper construction costs further west were an added incentive. Initially the plans caused disputes with landowners, particularly with Henry **Alexander** as he had to sacrifice both land and houses. Further west, especially in **Earl's Court**, tracks passed through rural land and the 'District' line was for some time virtually without traffic. Here the railway acted as a stimulus to building and was more warmly welcomed, especially by the ever debt-ridden Lord Kensington. Between 1868 and 1871 all the major landowners released land to the railway companies. Four stations, South Kensington, Gloucester Road, Earl's Court and West Brompton, were built, in addition to High Street Kensington, thus opening up the whole area.

Although the estate owners hoped that the railway would attract the 'carriage class' requiring large family houses and servants, instead it made the area more attractive to a more middle-class group of commuters. This had the effect of making the area less exclusive, especially in the west. The arrival of the Piccadilly line in 1906 further accelerated this process.

High Street Kensington station, designed by John Fowler, was opened in October 1868. In 1908 the iron frame and glass roof were demolished and a new station with a shopping arcade was opened – the arcade and booking hall were renovated in 1937 at a time when huge crowds used the station to go to the summer and winter sales at the High Street department stores. Recently refitted once more, the arcade is dominated by mobile phone shops, fast food outlets and fashion stores.

Gloucester Road, another John Fowler construction but this time with an upper storey and wings, also opened in 1868. During the refit to accommodate the Piccadilly line in 1905-6 the roof was removed but the façade was left intact. This was recently restored to its former glory.

South Kensington station, which had caused H B Alexander such problems in 1868, is once again causing great concern to local residents. This was one of the first stations to incorporate an arcade of shops – this is still in use today and retains its original fittings. The Piccadilly line extension was designed by Leslie Green, and the station's red terracotta-tiled façade contains Art Nouveau cartouches as well as distinctive black lettering on the lower frieze. Another unusual feature is the pedestrian tunnel built in 1885 to provide access to international exhibitions, the Royal Horticultural Gardens and the museums. This is an early example of a subway to take foot traffic – it also had electric lighting. In recognition of its historical status, in April 2006 the tunnel was listed despite its poor state of repair. It is hoped this will be rectified via a Lottery grant, thus becoming an integral part

158. Construction of Gloucester Road station.

159. South Kensington station, c.1905.

160. High Street Kensington station, soon after construction in 1868.

of the Exhibition Road project.

Development plans for the station, which included a multi-storied tower, have been mired in controversy for several years, the main objections being the sheer size of the project and that it does not match its environment. The recent listing of the station it is hoped will lead to a more sympathetic design.

The first Earl's Court station, built of wood, opened on the east side of the Earl's Court Road in 1871 but was destroyed in a fire in 1875. The new station, on its current site, was opened in 1878 with additional space for the extension to Putney Bridge. At Earl's Court the Piccadilly line was a deep-level tube and the station was rebuilt in 1915 with a more elegant façade but using a paler coloured tile. In 1936-7 an improved entrance was built onto the Warwick Road to serve the new Earl's Court Exhibition building.

It was here that the first escalator on the Underground was installed in 1911. 'Bumper' Harris, a war veteran with a wooden leg, was employed to ride up and down all day to demonstrate that it was safe. Extensive renovation is currently being undertaken.

West Brompton station opened in 1869 and abutted that of the West London Extension Railway which had opened three years earlier. The Railway was closed in 1940 and the station dismantled. A similar fate seemed to await the Underground station as services were restricted in the early 1990s. Instead the railway station was reconstructed and reopened and the the two are once again running in parallel.

Two new stations, **Brompton Road** and Knightsbridge on the Piccadilly line were opened on 15 December 1906. Both were designed by Leslie Green with round arched fronts clad with ox-blood tiles. Brompton Road station was closed in 1934.

United Reformed Church

Based in the Kensington Chapel in Allen Street this new group was formed when the Congregationalists, the original occupiers of the building, united with the Presbyterians who formerly worshipped at St John's Church, Scarsdale Villas. This followed the formation of the United Reformed Church in 1972.

In the middle of the 19th century when Nonconformist evangelism was at its height among the shop keeping and trading classes, part of the congregation of the Hornton Street Chapel determined to build a new and much larger chapel in Allen Street. In 1853 they moved into the new building with its four columned Corinthian façade. The chapel was soon filled with people from far and wide who came to hear the Rev C Silvestor Horne preach. He later went on to become an MP.

Damaged by a bomb in 1940, the building was not repaired until 1952 and it was then leased to the Catholic congregation of **Our Lady of Victories** whose church was being re-built. The United Reformed Church took over the building in 1975. In the 1990s extensive renovations were carried out which included cleaning the façade.

Vestry and Town Halls

In 1855 London government was restructured and civil vestries, elected by ratepayers, created. Both Kensington and its neighbour, Chelsea became metropolitan vestries with additional powers and functions. New Vestry Halls were required to reflect their new status and to accommodate the increased staff. The building of Kensington Vestry Hall on Kensington High Street led to accusations by ratepayers of extravagance. They accused the vestrymen of being more concerned with their accommodation and "gold lace on the Beadle's uniform" than the ratepayers.

The building was in reality quite modest and soon too small for the purpose. The decision to build a new Vestry Hall on the site of Hawksmoor's **Charity School** came in 1875. After an architectural competition, which caused the usual arguments and disagreements, the Vestrymen ignored the advisor they had called in, and chose Robert Walker. The foundation stone was laid in 1878 and the building was opened in 1880. It was described in *The Kensington Souvenir* in 1907 as "solid and substantial rather than original and handsome".

The old Vestry Hall was used to accommodate the new Central Library until 1960 and since then, apart from a short occupation by Bank Melli, the building has stood empty and deserted on the north side of the High Street. The second Hall was to suffer an even more ignominious end when it was demolished by the wrecking ball early in the hours of 11 June 1982.

161. *Kensington High Street c.1905. The old Vestry Hall became the Central Library, and beside it a new Town Hall for Kensington was built.*

When local government boundaries were redrawn Kensington and Chelsea were amalgamated, despite a long and hard battle against this fought by Chelsea residents. The Royal Borough of Kensington and Chelsea was created in 1965. It soon became apparent that the old Town Hall on Kensington High Street was too small, with many Council departments scattered around the borough. And so a large site just north of the High Street and behind the Central Library was acquired. Sir Basil Spence was commissioned to design a new building. Once again there was considerable dissent and a Public Enquiry was held before the foundations were laid in 1973. Kensington and Chelsea Town Hall and Civic Centre was opened on 31 May 1977.

Queen Victoria

Victoria (1819-1901), the daughter of the Duke of Kent and Princess Victoria of Saxe-Coburg, was born on 24 May 1819 in a dressing room in the north-east corner of the Palace.

Her christening in the Cupola Room on 24 June vividly shows the family disagreements and intrigue into which the young princess was born. The Duke had submitted to the Prince Regent the names Georgina Charlotte Augusta Alexandrina Victoria. The day before the christening Georgina was disallowed but no decision on the other names was given. The Archbishop with the Princess in his arms waited for the Regent to give her a name. At last he allowed Alexandrina, the Duke suggested Charlotte "No" replied the Regent, Augusta, "No" came the reply,

162. *A miniature painting of the young Victoria.*

Elizabeth, "No". By this time the Duchess was in tears, when the Regent finally shouted "Call her after her mother" thus the baby was christened Alexandrina Victoria.

The little Mayflower, as Victoria was known, became a familiar figure in Kensington Gardens riding in her pony and trap, a gift of the Duke of York. She was spoilt by her mother, had appalling table manners, shouted at the servants and was frightened of Uncle Sussex. Victoria remembered her childhood as being rather melancholy.

On a happier note it was here that she first met Prince Albert and was immediately smitten, describing him as "so handsome, so full of goodness and sweetness, and very clever and intelligent."

In the early hours of the morning of 21 June 1837 she was woken by her mother and told that she was Queen. She left Kensington Palace on the 13th of July confiding in her diary "it is not without regret that I bid adieu for ever … to this my birthplace … to which I am really attached".

Victoria & Albert Museum

The Museum of Manufactures, as the Victoria & Albert was initially known, was first established in Marlborough House. Helped by a government grant the collections were moved to a site on the north-east corner of Exhibition Road, which included Brompton Park House, and renamed the South Kensington Museum. The original building was very utilitarian and made mainly of corrugated iron, hence its popular name of 'the Brompton Boilers'.

Henry Cole was the first director and declared that the Museum should be a 'schoolroom for everyone'. In the month following the opening by Queen Victoria on 24 June 1857 there were over 14,000 visitors.

As the collections grew, extensions were erected and in 1890 Aston Webb won the competition to design a new entrance and façade for the museum now to be renamed Victoria & Albert at the expressed wish of the Queen. The completed building was opened by King Edward VII in 1909.

Today the V & A is the country's foremost museum of applied arts. New or re-vamped galleries are constantly being added such as the British Galleries and the latest featuring Islamic art. Despite all the improvements and additions, at its core, surrounding a central garden, lie the original mid-Victorian galleries with their magnificent terracotta reliefs.

Jubal Webb

Cheesemonger Jubal Webb (d. 1901) was a shopkeeper with influence in local affairs and on the development of Kensington. Initially based on the south side of the High Street, he moved in

163. The 'Brompton Boilers' – the first building of the Victoria & Albert Museum – from the Illustrated London News *in June 1857.*

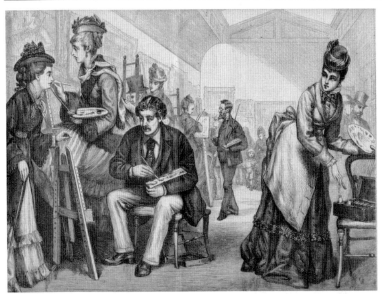

164. *Students drawing and painting at the South Kensington Museum. From the* Pictorial World, *January 1875.*

the 1860s to a site next to **St Mary Abbots Church.** His telegraphic address was 'Gorgonzola, London'. He was a long serving vestryman, a member of the Metropolitan Board of Works and a churchwarden.

In 1893 he exhibited an enormous cheese weighing 22,000 pounds at the Chicago World Fair – its transportation presented all sorts of difficulties. It was later returned to England where it was served at a banquet, by which time it must have been very ripe.

Webb took a house in the Terrace in the High Street and when the surrounding land came up for sale he purchased it for £170,000. First, he built a promenade of new shops, now 129-161 Kensington High Street, which he promptly sold to the Crown. He then went on to develop the rest of the site. Here Iverna Court and Iverna Mansions were built from 1894. Sadly his plans to build a theatre in 'the very best theatrical style and in keeping with the

traditions of Kensington as the Royal Suburb' were never realised. The proposed site was eventually used instead by **St Sarkis Armenian Church** and the Christian Science Church.

West London Air Terminal

The Cromwell Curve, a triangular piece of land between Cromwell Road, Lexham Gardens and Emperor's Gate where the District and Circle lines intersect, was rafted over in the mid 20th century. The West London Air Terminal was built over it. From here passengers could book in for their flights and be whisked by coach to and from Heathrow Airport, unencumbered by luggage. But as passenger numbers grew and traffic conditions worsened the terminal was no longer viable and the site was sold. The front part of the site was taken by Sainsbury's and Point West was constructed at the rear.

White Eagle Lodge

The studio and animal painting school of the artist W Frank Calderon, built in 1910 in St Mary Abbots Place, was taken over after the Second World War by a charitable religious trust, White Eagle Lodge.

In the early 1930s, two spiritual missions based in Bayswater drew audiences to hear the psychic teaching of White Eagle, a Red Indian Chief, through the medium, Grace Cooke, known as Minesta. Later, at Pembroke Hall, the Cookes' clairvoyance was combined with spiritual healing. After the war, together with her husband Ivan, known as Brother Faithfull, and a large group of members, the move to St Mary Abbots Place was made.

Since then new lodges have been established in many parts of the UK, including the White Temple in Liss, Hampshire, and abroad. Today their activities include meditation and healing, the organisation of retreats and courses in subjects such as yoga and astrology as well as regular services of worship and communion.

William III and Mary II

The Glorious Revolution of 1688 brought the Protestant William of Orange (1650-1702), grandson of Charles I, and Mary (1662-1694), daughter of James II to the British throne. Their reign was turbulent and neither was popular. They, especially William, were seen to be distant and aloof and William found among the English "an incorrigible slowness and negligence". Despite this, with the signing of the Bill of Rights they were to leave a

165. William III, from the oil painting by W. Wissing.

166. Queen Mary, from a painting by P. Lilly.

lasting legacy. Britain had become a Great Power, with a sound financial system and Parliament was firmly established with the fear of absolute rule eradicated.

It was in their private lives, especially at Kensington, that they found great happiness. William was asthmatic, and the fog rising from the Thames was bad for his health so they set out to find a more suitable winter palace than Whitehall. They settled on Nottingham House, home of Sir Heneage Finch and commanded Sir Christopher Wren to improve the house with all haste. They took up residence in Christmas 1689 and were delighted with their new home, **Kensington Palace**.

Further improvements followed including the Route de Roi, a straight, wide road, lit by lamps to deter footpads, from the Palace to Hyde Park, part of which can be seen in Rotten Row today. Extensive work was undertaken in the gardens by London and Wise of Brompton Park and the grounds were laid out in the Dutch style similar to Het Loo, William's favourite residence in Holland. Sadly, little trace of this remains as Queen Anne detested the smell of box and had it all dug up. The creation of this garden was to be Mary's great solace during William's frequent military excursions abroad, unhappiness owing to his relationship with Elizabeth Villiers and her own

frequent miscarriages. Mary died in 1694 from smallpox and William in 1702 following a fall from his horse at Hampton Court. They were succeeded by Queen Anne, Mary's sister.

Emlyn Williams

George Emlyn Williams (1905-1987) was the archetypal Welsh scholarship boy, who won a place at Christ Church, Oxford and then on graduation chose the uncertainties of repertory theatre. Initially an actor, he had his first success as a dramatist when he was just twenty-five and confirmed his reputation with two plays which became standard – the grisly chiller *Night Must Fall* (1935) and *The Corn is Green* (1938), a semi-autobiographical exploration of the relationship between a young Welsh miner and his female teacher. By the time Williams was living at 15 Pelham Crescent between 1953 and 1960, he had developed a new career, giving public readings as Charles Dickens. In 1955 he switched to reading Dylan Thomas, re-enacting the poet's autobiographical account of his Swansea childhood in *A Boy Growing Up*. It was also during this period that Williams composed his own autobiography, *George,* which was published in 1961.

Woolsthorpe House

Like so many other Kensington mansions Woolsthorpe House in Wright's Lane was converted into a school; but in this case, rather unusually, into a home for 'crippled boys'.

Built by Gregory Wright in the 1760s it was named in honour of Sir Issac Newton whose birthplace was Woolsthorpe in Lincolnshire. Newton owned but never lived in a property on Wright's Lane.

The National Industrial Home for Crippled Boys was founded in 1869. The charity, under the presidency of the Earl of Shaftesbury, converted and enlarged the mansion to include workshops, schoolrooms, dormitories and an infirmary. Here about sixty boys between the ages of 12 and 18 were taught the relatively sedentary trades of printing, tailoring and shoemaking.

After the First World War there was a decline in entrants, so in 1935 the site was sold and the proceeds used towards the building of the Royal National Orthopaedic Hospital at Stanmore. Kensington Close Hotel, built in 1936, now occupies the site.

167. Emlyn Williams.

Yeats family

In 1887, 58 Eardley Crescent was briefly occupied by the Irish painter John Butler Yeats and his two talented sons, Jack B, the future painter, and William Butler, the future poet and Nobel Laureate. Their sister Lily thought the house horrible and dismissed its garden as a '"bit of cat-haunted sooty gravel". The boys however were much happier as they got free tickets for Buffalo Bill's show at the newly opened Earl's Court Exhibition, though the constant gunfire did disturb the family's sleep. By 1888 the family had moved to Bedford Park.

Yeoman's Row

By the 1850s 34 cottages had been built along the west side of Yeoman's Row. These were mainly occupied by the working classes, adding to those built on the eastern side in the 1770s. The 1851 census shows that 1,020 inhabitants were living in 68 little houses, an average of fifteen in each; one even had six

168. Yeoman's Row.

separate families with a total of twenty-eight people. By 1881 this had only dropped to an average of thirteen per house. A far cry from the occupancy of these now highly desirable residencies today.

The process of change began in the 1890s with the construction of studios on the west side. The tension between residents came to a head in 1931 when the London County Council took action to clear the various sheds and pigeon-houses on the forecourt of Grove Cottages. One studio owner wrote, 'the majority of the people here are a very ignorant and dirty crowd' and complained of quarrelsome dogs and cats. Only numbers 27 to 33 survived the subsequent gentrification of the east side. One person at least mourned their passing, John Betjeman, who described the cottages as 'the last glimpse of the village of Brompton when it stood in the market gardens of Knightsbridge'.

It is worth mentioning one more survivor, the Bunch of Grapes pub which sits on the corner of Yeoman's Row and Brompton Road. The pub was built in 1770 and rather unusually has retained its name. It was owned by Sir Swinnerton Dyer and Baroness van Zandt before it was rebuilt in 1844. Many of the features from this time remain including the 'snob' screens which separated the gentlemen from the working class locals, the front bow window, etched glass and mirrors, wood panelling and the ornate Corinthian pillars around the bar.

Thomas Young

It was the dream of Thomas Young, a woodcarver in the tradition of Grinling Gibbons, to produce a beautiful residential square in the fields near the old parish church of St Mary Abbots. Young is believed to have been born in Devon, and was apprenticed to a joiner and woodcarver, being admitted as a freeman of the Joiners' Company in 1670 when he was about twenty. He was one of the woodcarvers employed by Wren in rebuilding the City churches. It soon became clear that he was an artist and craftsman but not a business man.

Kensington Square was the first venture on his own, undertaken in 1685, and this may explain his subsequent financial difficulties. Eventually he was forced to sell part of the land to other builders, retaining six sites for himself. Here, between Spring Garden and Bowling Green he built a twelve-roomed Bowling Green House, where he lived with his wife and children. He continued to borrow money and was later arrested for debt and imprisoned in the King's Bench Prison.

While there he was persuaded by Thomas Sutton, his backer, to hand over more equity including the Bowling Green to prevent other creditors seizing his remaining plots and to secure his release. This left Sutton in possession of the freeholds. When Young left prison he was unable to raise a loan to repay Sutton, got back into debt and languished in Fleet prison for nearly ten years. Eventually he brought a case against Sutton in the Chancery complaining that Sutton had "quite digged up" the Bowling Green and garden.

Zetland Arms

This pub stands on the corner of Bute Street and Old Brompton Road and dates from the mid 1840s. Bute Street was laid out in the grounds of Bute House, a villa built for his own use in 1770 by the architect James Adam, brother of the more famous Robert Adam.

The pub and its counterpart are the only survivors of the mid 1840s development. The northern end of Bute Street was swept away when the District Railway was constructed under what was to become Harrington Road. The rest was reconstructed as modest residences with shops below between 1953 and 1966. The most common language spoken in Bute Street is French as most of the shops and cafés cater for the large French population of the area, attracted by the nearby Lycée Charles de Gaulle and the **French Institute**.

The pub was built by Edwin Curtis and externally, especially on the upper floors, remains relatively unchanged as does the name. A board outside the pub claims that it comes from the Danish influence in the area at that time. One further item of note is the name of the proprietor in the 1880; it was Syd Chaplin, half brother of Charlie. Charlie and Sydney, who later became his business manger, were born into poverty in Lambeth and ended up in an institute for destitute children when their parents separated shortly after Charlie's birth. Recently a home movie shot by Sydney, during the making of Charlie Chaplin's first talking picture *The Great Dictator*, was shown on television.

Further Reading

Clunn, Harold, *The Face of London* (1932 rev. 1972)

Barbara Denny and Carolyn Starren, *Kensington Past* (1998)

Barbara Denny and Carolyn Starren, *Kensington and Chelsea in Old Photographs* (1996)

Andrew Duncan, *Secret London* (1995)

Thomas Faulkner, *History of Antiquities of Kensington* (1820)

Rachael Ferguson, *Royal Borough* (1950)

Judith Flanders *The Victorian House* (2003)

John Glanfield, *Earls Court and Olympia* (2003)

The Hill, Local History articles (1986-2004)

Derek Hudson, *Kensington Palace* (1968)

Leigh Hunt, *The Old Court Suburb* (1855)

Kensington Local Studies cuttings collection

Kensington News 1869-1998 (Barbara Denny files)

Kensington Society Annual Reports 1954-2005

W J Loftie, *Kensington Picturesque and Historical* (1888)

London Transport, *100 years of the District* (1968)

Shirley Nicholson, *A Victorian Household* (1988)

D W Peel, *Garden in the Sky: the Story of Barkers* (1960)

Lord Ponsonby of Shulbrede, *Records of Kensington Square* (1987)

Barbara Rosen and Wolfgang Zuckermann, *Mews of London* (1982)

Survey of London Vol. XXXVIII: *The Museums Area of South Kensington* (1975)

Survey of London Vol. XLI *South Kensington: Brompton* (1983)

Survey of London Vol. XLII *Southern Kensington from Kensington Square to Earl's Court* (1886)

Richard Tames, *Earl's Court and Brompton Past* (2000)

Annabel Walker with Peter Jackson, *Kensington and Chelsea: a social and architectural history* (1987)

Giles Walkley, *Artists' Houses in London 1764-1914* (1994)

Ben Weinreb and Christopher Hibbert (editors), *The London Encyclopaedia* (Rev. edition 1993)

E J Willson, *West London Nursery Gardens* (1982)

Useful websites

www.londonfacet.net

www.rbkc.gov.uk/virtualmuseum

www.victorianlondon.org

www.victorianweb.org

Index

Asterisks denote illustration or caption